Alexandre Brou, Alexandre Brou

Saint Augustine Of Canterbury And His Companions

Alexandre Brou, Alexandre Brou

Saint Augustine Of Canterbury And His Companions

ISBN/EAN: 9783743462861

Manufactured in Europe, USA, Canada, Australia, Japa

Cover: Foto ©ninafisch / pixelio.de

Manufactured and distributed by brebook publishing software (www.brebook.com)

Alexandre Brou, Alexandre Brou

Saint Augustine Of Canterbury And His Companions

St. Martin's Church, Canterbury.

SAINT AUGUSTINE

OF CANTERBURY

AND HIS COMPANIONS

From the French of
FATHER BROU, S.J.

Dies nostros in tua pace disponas
Words added by Saint Gregory
the Great to the Canon Missæ

LONDON AND LEAMINGTON
ART AND BOOK COMPANY
LONDON: CATHOLIC TRUTH SOCIETY
NEW YORK, CINCINNATI, CHICAGO: BENZIGER BROTHERS
1897

Nihil obstat:
> HERBERTUS THURSTON, S.J.

Imprimatur:
> ✠ EDUARDUS,
> > EPISCOPUS BIRMINGHAMIENSIS.

Die 1º Septembris, 1897.

NOTE

THE publishers wish to record their thanks to Father Thurston, S.J., for his kindness in reading the proofs of the English edition of this work and for other help in connection with it. They are especially indebted to him for light he has thrown on liturgical and kindred questions.

Some effort and haste has been necessary to bring out the work in time for the centenary celebration of St. Augustine, with which it coincides in the date of its appearance. Although care has been taken to verify every statement of importance contained in the French edition, it is possible that some errors have remained undiscovered. The publishers will be grateful if any that may be found be reported to them.

PREFACE

THE following pages tell the story of a great undertaking rather than describe a saint's life, and St. Gregory rather than his missionary St. Augustine holds the chief place of honour. The conversion of the Anglo-Saxons was the brightest ornament of that great pope's reign ; or at least it is that which the Church seems to prize above all the rest, for to this day, three hundred years after the great revolt, St. Gregory is still described in the Roman Martyrology as he " who brought the English to the true faith."

Of St. Augustine himself, the chief lieutenant of the papacy in its conquest of England, but little is known. His life and his virtues are overshadowed by his mission. That mission dates from the abortive schemes of St. Gregory while still a monk, and ends with the death of the last Italian archbishop of Canterbury. It is that period which I have included in my sketch.

Perhaps it was rash of me to undertake the task ; for Montalembert has already told the same story, and he is a bold man who would invite comparison with the glowing pages of *The Monks of the West*. Yet the critical value of that work has been denied : I think with justice. The passionate soul of the orator not unnaturally chafes at the restrictions imposed upon the student of history, though the historian who fears to pall by the dulness of his own pages may well envy the tender but stirring narrative of Montalembert.

So I have sought to tell again in my own way what Montalembert has told so well already. Moreover the occasion seemed favourable, for while France was holding festival at Rheims in memory of the conversion of Clovis, on the other side of the Channel Catholics and Protestants alike were thinking of St. Augustine and the baptism of Ethelbert. English Catholics are about to hold their commemoration of that event on the very ground where the saint is believed to have landed with his monks. The Anglicans have already held theirs. The occasion happily concurred with the celebration of the diamond jubilee of the queen's reign; and nearly two hundred Protestant bishops gathered in synod from every part of the British empire. They had held such meetings before, and it was easy to anticipate that those prelates would have a difficulty in finding a common ground for debate in which their differences should not too much obtrude. We knew they would discuss reunion, and they could not wholly ignore the appeal of the holy see. Could they fail to draw a comparison in their own minds between pope Gregory who sent England the faith, and pope Leo who invites her to reunion?

Could they fail to recognize that at an interval of thirteen centuries there breathes in the utterances of Leo the same spirit that inspired the action of Gregory? " Father, ... that they may be one ! "

I write these lines at the very spot where of old St. Augustine lived. For many years past I have lived at Canterbury, a place still rich in traces of the saints who worked and died there. The little city is full of memories of her lost greatness. There preached England's first archbishop; there dwelt a long line of holy prelates ; the pavement of the cathedral was once smeared with a martyr's blood; in her archbishop's palace was reared another Thomas, likewise a martyr, though he won his crown elsewhere—he too was chancellor, but to another Henry. A thoughtful Catholic who lives at such a place must regard with ever growing affection those witnesses to the past; but his affection will be tinged with sadness. How few of those that visit Canterbury feel aught save a certain antiquarian regret as they look at the crumbling ruins of her abbeys! How few ever picture to themselves the life of the great past of which those ruins stand in silent record !

To link the Church of the nineteenth century with that of the seventh there is at Canterbury but a handful of Catholics, chiefly Irish, who are joined at Sunday mass by an occasional visitor from the continent. In the great metropolitan church there is scarcely a stone which does not mourn for the banished faith. Within its walls a Catholic feels like a disinherited son returning after long absence to his ancestral home.

Though the present tenants of Christchurch have held possession for three hundred years, they have not yet made themselves at home there. It is so manifest that the place was not built for them; nave and choir are too long and too wide; on every side are chapels in which of old mass was offered daily, for which they have now no use. Their services are held apart in a mere corner of the great building; the rest they leave to the tourist.

Once a year the liberal spirit of the Anglican canons throws the church open to Catholic pilgrims. They are permitted to kneel there, say their beads and make their *private* devotions. Once even they were allowed to have a meeting in the chapter-house. On such occasions they fill the railway-station, wearing their badges, and parade through the city with banners flying. Instead of insult or ridicule they meet with civility and respect. Who knows but that God will some day be moved by the prayers of those devout souls who flock hither to honour the soil once trodden by His saints?

PRINCIPAL WORKS CONSULTED

S. Gregorii Epistolæ. (Monumenta Germaniæ Historica.)
Bede. Historia Ecclesiastica.
Goscelin. Vita S. Augustini; Miracula. (Acta SS. Maii 26.)
Paulus Diaconus, et Joannes Diaconus. Vita S. Gregorii. (Migne, P. L.)
Thomas de Elmham and W. Thorn. Historia Monast. S. Augustini.
The Anglo-Saxon Chronicle.
Willis. Architectural History of Canterbury Cathedral. (London, 1845.)
,, Architectural History of the Conventual Buildings of the Monastery of Christ Church.
Haddan and Stubbs. Councils and Ecclesiastical Documents.
Dean Hook. Lives of the Archbishops of Canterbury.
Dean Stanley. Memorials of Canterbury.
Canon Mason. The Mission of St. Augustine.
F. Oakeley. Life of St. Augustine. (Lives of Eng. SS.)
J. R. Green. The Making of England.
J. Morris, S.J. Canterbury: Our Old Metropolis.

CONTENTS

CHAPTER		Page
I	Celts and Saxons	1
II	St. Gregory	18
III	St. Augustine's Mission	30
IV	Canterbury	51
V	St. Gregory's Letters	67
VI	The Welsh Church	95
VII	Augustine's Last Years and Death	115
VIII	St. Augustine's Work under his Immediate Successors	131
IX	St. Paulinus of York	140
X	Gloria Posthuma	171

LIST OF ILLUSTRATIONS

St. Martin's Church, Canterbury		*Frontispiece*
Gateway, St. Augustine's Abbey	*To face page*	62
Plan of Canterbury Cathedral in Saxon Times	,, ,,	64
Canterbury Cathedral from the North-East	*Page*	182

The figure of St. Augustine on the cover is reproduced from that designed by A. W. Pugin for F. Oakeley's "St. Augustine" *in* "Lives of English Saints."

ST. AUGUSTINE
OF CANTERBURY

Chapter I—CELTS AND SAXONS

I

THE SAXON invasion of Britain began about the year 450. Some fifty years later the places where the invaders had disembarked or which they had first won from the natives were still mere isolated stations lying at intervals along the island's eastern and southern coasts. In the middle of the sixth century these little centres so grew in extent as to reach from one to the other; and thus the Teutonic races became possessed of territory forming a broad, irregular, but almost unbroken band compassing nearly half the island. Fresh hordes still kept pouring in across the seas. The stream flowed unceasingly, until certain districts of Germany were stripped of their inhabitants. Kent was so thoroughly mastered that not a Briton remained, although it had taken nearly ten years to annihilate the Celtic population and to dislodge them from their strongholds in the forest of Anderida. Twenty-six years passed before Wessex was established in the south; and then in that part of the island the tide of invasion ceased for half a century. On the eastern coast the German tribes still flowed in, bringing with them their wives and flocks. The natives were gradually driven back into the interior, so that about the middle of the sixth century they only held the Thames valley as far as London.

In the beginning at least the invasion was terribly fierce. The Britons had recovered something of their former spirit, and by their resistance exasperated their Jute and Saxon enemies. Unfortunately those who should have been united in defending their homes against the common foe were perhaps even more lacking in concert than the invaders themselves. Just as each of the German chieftains acted for his private ends, so did those petty British princes give heed only to their own personal danger. The story of their defence against the Romans was repeated. They made heroic efforts; but their bravery was rendered unavailing by their heedlessness and selfishness. Not till they saw the Saxons gain point after point before their very eyes were they roused from their stolid indifference.

Gildas the monk observed from his retreat in Wales the ever-victorious progress of the enemy. "Just vengeance for our people's former sins!" he cried in his own weird style; "from sea to sea spread the fire kindled in the east, fed by sacrilegious hands, laying waste town and country-side, only staying its course when, after withering well-nigh the whole face of our island, it licked with its fierce red tongue the western ocean. Towns crumbled into ruins beneath the battering-ram; and they that dwelt therein with their bishops, their clergy and all their people . . . amid the flash of swords and crackling of the flames fell dead to the ground. Oh, the horror of that sight! In the public squares lay the gateways wrenched from their hinges, stones from the city walls, consecrated altars, mangled corpses weltering in red pools of clotted gore, all mingled in dire confusion, as though crunched together by some horrible machine. Their tombs were the ruined houses or the bellies of wild beasts or birds of prey; save only the souls of the saints, if perchance there were found any in those dread times whom the angels might bear aloft to heaven. How many poor wretches were pursued to the mountains and there massacred in troops! Others dying of starvation delivered themselves up to a life-long slavery, if they might not perish on the spot, the boon they craved most. Others passed over the sea with loud lamentations, and beneath the swelling sails they sang: *Thou hast given us like sheep to be eaten; Thou hast scattered us amongst the gentiles.** Others again, entrenched within the mountains, behind sheer precipices, or sheltered by dense forests or the cliffs by the sea, ever watchful and trembling, yet hopeful, forsook not their fatherland."

It is said that traces of these poor refugees are still found in certain caves near Settle in Yorkshire. The different layers of the rubbish there accumulated bear witness to the sad fate of those that there sought shelter. First the hyena came to devour limbs of bears, or bisons, or mammoths; next came a race of savages, armed with flint hatchets and arrows of bone. Long after these had passed away came the British refugees, driving before them their cattle, swine and goats, "whose bones lie scattered round the hearth-fire at the mouth of the cave, where they served the wretched fugitives for food. . . . At night-fall all were crouching beneath the dripping roof of the cave or round the fire that was blazing at its mouth, and a long suffering began in which the fugitives lost year by year the memory of the civilization from which they came." †

At that period Britain was in a sad plight. In no other part of Europe had the existing civilization vanished so

---

* Ps. xliii. 4. † J. R. Green, *The Making of England*, c. ii.

completely before the inroads of barbarism. It is true that what civilization there was, was slight and superficial; Romans and Celts had not mixed much together. The conquering nation had built little save garrison towns, fortresses and camps. Except in London, Verulam, Colchester, York, and other great military stations or centres of commerce, where a mixed race had grown up and formed the bulk of the population, the Britons for the most part held sullenly aloof; they were ever ready to give secret assistance to the Picts, who would constantly force their way within the great walls in the north and descend as far as the Thames. Save for a few isolated Roman stations the island was much as it had been in the past. Vast wildernesses lay between the towns; the Roman roads traversed the country, passing by forest, moor and fenland, the lair of the wild bull and the wolf. There also lived the Britons in solitary huts, a race of shepherds, little better than savages, who still spoke their own language and kept their own laws; a hardy people, but quite incapable of political life.

What was the fate of the old Roman and British cities during the invasion? In some cases, as at Deva or Anderida, the population was annihilated. Deva rose up again in later years, but nothing was known of Anderida * save the square mass of masonry which forms its ruins. In the twelfth century it was a mere heap of stones without a single inhabitant. Other towns had so completely disappeared that till a little while ago no one knew where to look for their traces.

Calleva Atrebatum was not a military station, hemmed in like Lincoln by strong fortifications, but a commercial city of some extent, boasting of a forum, with streets and suburbs, which lay quite unprotected by citadel or walls. How and when did she fall? Recent years have

* Pevensey.

again brought her to light under the foundations of modern Silchester, with her Christian church and a wall hastily set up on the very eve of the enemy's approach.

Uriconium * met with a similar fate; but we know the date of her fall—A.D. 583. She was even greater than London in Roman times, and the British bard sang of her as "the white town in the valley, the town of white stones gleaming among the green woodland." When the bard went back to her, he found only a mass of charred ruins. Her palaces were "without fire, light, or song," their stillness was broken only by the eagle's scream, the eagle "who has swallowed fresh drink, heart's blood of Kyndylan the fair."† Uriconium also has been excavated. When discovered, her wide streets were still strewn with bones, and human skeletons were found even in the warming chambers of her baths and houses.

Other towns were afterwards restored. Towards the seventh century Winchester rose upon the site of Guenta Belgarum. During the eighth century Cambridge was still a mere heap of ruins. The military station of Deva remained for four centuries a nameless solitude, spoken of as the "waste camp," ‡ till it was restored under the vague name of Chester—the camp, *castra*. York was not built on the old site of Eburacum till the days of Canute. The London of the Angles did not reach the importance it had enjoyed under the Romans till just before the Norman conquest. The small plot of ground enclosed by the walls of Durovernum was yet a good deal too wide for Saxon Canterbury.

* Wroxeter.
† Llywarch Hen, apud J. R. Green, *The Making of England*, c. v.
‡ "On an wæstre ceastre."—Angl. Sax. Chron. A.D. 894.

II

MEANWHILE the Church was swept away with the rest. Hitherto the Church in Britain had been the only abiding monument of the Roman occupation; she alone had survived the departure of the legions. Her bishops sat at the councils of Arles and Sardica, and submitted like the rest to the papal legates. They were poor men, for at the synod of Rimini they alone had boarded at the cost of the emperor Constantius. They had kept up communion with the continental Churches and especially with Rome so far as was permitted by their remote situation at the very limits of the inhabited world. In other countries people were not unmindful of the existence of the British Church; and when a learned writer wished to describe the Church's victories, it was to Britain that he turned: the faith had penetrated even to Britain! In Britain the Church had had her martyrs—first and foremost amongst them St. Alban. The arch-heretic Pelagius also had been one of her children. Monasticism flourished in her bosom. The popes and her sister-Churches in Gaul watched her with kindly interest, and sent her apostles and reformers, such as German of Auxerre, Victricius of Rouen, Ninian, Palladius, and Patrick. She possessed organisation and life of her own.

Yet even she was carried away by the torrent. Her sacred buildings were burnt or pulled down, or devoted to the idolatrous worship of her enemies. "The priests were slain," says Venerable Bede; "the bishop and his flock were driven forth by fire and sword, and none remained to bury the maimed bodies of the dead." Then began the emigration of monks, laymen and bishops, which bore the remnants of the scattered Church to Armorica, and even into Spain. Soldiers and bards, chieftains at the head of their clans, abbots with their monks put to sea in frail barks, carrying away whatever property was left to them. A new country was founded which received the name of that from which they had fled. Hermits driven forth from their solitude sought a more peaceful retreat beyond the sea, and were sometimes raised to be bishops ere they found one. The exiles left with heartfelt grief, and the Bretons of Armorica long remembered the land whence they were sprung. "We still tarry in France," wrote Radbad, bishop of Dol, some three hundred years later, "in exile and captivity."

The few Britons that remained were treated as slaves and pariahs. These were most numerous in the western portion of the island. The Saxons naturally spared, whenever they might safely do so, as many men as would serve to work and till their newly won territory. It has been noticed that neither in standard English nor in its provincial dialects are there any words of Celtic origin concerned with legislation or war, or denoting articles of luxury. Some British words, however, of grosser meaning, and terms relating to husbandry, the crafts and home life were adopted by the conquerors. Without entering here upon a controversy which has been warmly debated it is clear that there still remained a few relics of the native population. For long afterwards these were distinguished from the race of their masters by the low *wergeld* at which their lives were assessed.

Did these captive Britons retain the faith when they became the slaves of their captors? In order to belittle the part played by our saint in England's conversion and to force a relationship between the present Anglican establishment and the old British Church—to which without any sufficient reason they attribute an eastern origin, independent of Rome—certain writers have alleged that St. Augustine and his Italian monks merely built anew on foundations that were already laid; that the Saxons had not exterminated the ancient race, and that the work of conversion was comparatively easy, since a kind of Christianity lay smouldering beneath the ruins, only waiting to be rekindled. There is, however, no evidence that the missionaries from Rome ever found in Saxon England a trace of any such dormant embers of the old religion. Neither is it certain that marriages with native women were frequent, or that the barbarians entertained so great an admiration for Rome as to make them the least bit more ready to adopt the faith of the vanquished.* Even had the Britons remained Christians, owing to their lot as slaves they could not have exercised any religious influence over their proud captors. Three-fourths of Britain became heathen, as though the faith had never yet been preached there.†

Very few are the material remains which survive from those days. Here and there may be found a cross, a tomb, an inscription, a few traces of a Christian church. At Canterbury there exists a most precious relic of the banished faith in the little church of St. Martin. I know no spot in England so suggestive to the Catholic heart as those four walls in spite of the restorations of succeeding ages. Glastonbury standing in solitary grandeur with many an old Celtic legend clinging about its ruins, and perhaps also the Tower of London with its stories of bloodshed and martyrdom, alone thrill the heart with such sad eloquence.

St. Martin's is merely a little parish church standing in one of the poorer parts of the town. The learned are divided concerning the true date of its foundation. Bede speaks of an ancient church lying to the east of the city, and dedicated in his day to the holy bishop of Tours, and tradition has it that it has endured to the present time.

* Cf. Hook's *Lives of the Archbishops*, i. pp. 44-6.
† Duchesne, *Églises Séparées*, pp. 7 sqq.

Celts and Saxons

For more than three hundred years the cold worship of Anglicanism has replaced the Mass offered on the spot by St. Augustine's predecessors and by St. Augustine himself. The sanctuary lamp which was tended with so much care till the very eve of the reformation will perhaps never shine there again. To most visitors it is merely a curious relic of an age long since passed away.*

Each succeeding century has left its mark upon the fabric. The Romans probably built the chief part of its walls. Their work may be recognised by the bricks built in with the flints, and by their mortar, made from sea-sand full of tiny pebbles and shells, which is much stronger than that used by Saxons or Normans. The chancel is Saxon work; so is the rudely cut font. The Normans raised the massive arches with their coarse mouldings. Later on the windows were enlarged; their tracery dates from the fourteenth or fifteenth century. The big square tower, now clad in a thick vesture of ivy, was built in the fifteenth century. Lastly in our own times much that was covered up has been excavated, and much that was perishing has been restored.

In the country round there is something to recall the past at every step. The slopes of yonder hill were once covered with Roman villas. The road which passes by its side was once lined with tombs. Those two fine towers were raised up in Saxon times and mark the entrance to St. Augustine's abbey, the mother-house of English monasteries. The apse of the cathedral church is Norman and existed in Lanfranc's day. Often portions date from the time of Anselm, or Thomas, or Edmund. The tall central tower with its bold presence yet simple lines marks the period of the Church's greatest temporal splendour, when England was spread with the geometrical tracery of her

* See *The History of St. Martin's Church*, by G. C. F. Routledge. (London, 1891.)

national Gothic. Ugly modern buildings now meet the eye where the abbey-church of St. Augustine once rose with nave and aisles as wide and tall as those of a cathedral—sad witness to an age when bishops fell away and monks were weak, and when at Canterbury a few mendicant friars alone were found worthy to be hanged or burnt for the faith of Rome. The spot brings back to memory these martyrs of a later date also; for behind the trees on the left is the British tumulus—now forming a portion of a public pleasure ground—where Blessed John Stone, the Augustinian monk, was hanged by order of Henry VIII. Close at hand is Oaten Hill, where three priests and a layman of Canterbury perished under Elizabeth.

The little church also suggests a thought about the future. In the narrow country churchyard which surrounds it, clergymen, bishops and soldiers have chosen to rest. The white crosses which mark their graves rise close together side by side. This choice of so lonely a spot in the city suburb marks the love for long past ages which lies deep in the hearts of many English churchmen. May it lead them back some day to that faith which alone has received the promise of everlasting life and alone preserves the deposit of unfailing tradition.

A new race had now settled in Britain, bringing with it from the shores of Germany its own political and social methods, its own customs and its own religion. The chiefs who had first established themselves in the island became kings. Then there sprang up a complicated machinery of local government, embracing the *gemot* or council of the village, the hundred-moot, the shire-moot, the witenagemot, or king's council of wise men. The soil was parcelled out; whatever remained after each family had received its share became common land.

There were no longer any large towns. The German,

Tacitus tells us, preferred to live alone, and therefore the Roman cities remained in great part unoccupied. Villages large and small grew up on the country-side. War was the Saxon's favourite pastime; his days were chiefly spent either in attacking or defending. The wealthy fortified their dwellings, while the villages and farms were protected by earthworks surmounted by a palisade or quickset hedge. Feuds would arise between one lord and another, or between neighbouring villages. Even the freemen, who suffered their hair to grow long and fall about their shoulders as a sign of independence, had a right to engage in private warfare.

The story of the Saxon conquest shows us what barbarism really meant. These men were pirates and thieves; they sacked and plundered; their cruelty was revolting; they shared the vices of those other turbulent races which for many centuries had been a scourge to the ancient world. In their Saxon homes they were neither better nor worse than the Franks and Burgundians, though they had a slight advantage in never having had contact with Roman civilisation.

When the stress of conquest was over, or nearly so, their fierce characters became somewhat tamer. When kingdoms were established in comparative peace and laws began to be administered, their manners softened. The Jutes, who had been so terrible a century and a half ago, seem to have made tractable and peaceful subjects under king Ethelbert, though they still remained pagans. Perhaps their neighbourhood with the Franks and their trade with the continent had brought them indirectly under some slight Christian influence. In their German fatherland they had been mere warriors and rovers by land or sea. They now settled upon the land, lost all taste for piracy, and became wealthy. They never cared for husbandry, but their wealth enabled them to employ slaves to till the soil. Their taste for war they never lost, and it found abundant scope in their own domestic quarrels.

Saxon literature throws a vivid light upon their character. Their paganism made them take a sad and gloomy view of life. If ever they thought of heaven, it was a kind of German beershop that they pictured to themselves, where they might sit drinking all day long, reclining on thrones in a vast hall. Their fancy loved to roam over seas that washed dismal island shores, where dwarfs and giants dwelt among ghosts and dragons and gnomes; or they would dream of climes where crows filled the air with their cries and eagles flew by bearing carrion in their beaks; of captured enemies flung into ditches filled with hissing serpents; of meals of human flesh; of battlefields running with human blood.

Such was the train of thought which runs through the poetry which has survived from their day; and their ideals were well-nigh realized in their actual lives. Their history is a long continuous tale of assassinations and slaughter. For many years they were best known by their piracies; they were the scourge of the northern seas. In their flat-bottomed boats they would land on any suitable shore and row up rivers heedless of shoal or sandbank. Their galleys of oak carried not merely the crew but bands of warriors as well, armed with spears, long arrows and knives. Sometimes they put to sea in a frailer vessel still—a mere wicker basket covered with hide. By means of these they inspired terror into the western ports. Their favourite quarry was human life, and they pursued it with every refinement of cruelty.*

Take the list of Northumbrian kings during the eighth century; out of fifteen princes only two died peaceful deaths. Erdwulf was driven into exile; Osred fell victim

* Cf. Sidon. Apoll., Ep. viii. 6, carm. vii.; Green's *Making of England*, p. 18, note 2.

to a conspiracy; Osric was slain; Ceolwulf was captured, stripped of his possessions and made to abdicate; Oswulf was slain by members of his own house; Ailred and Ethelred were exiled; Elfwald was overthrown and slain by a conspiracy; Osred was made prisoner, banished and then slain; Ethelred, after being restored, was slain by his own subjects; Oswald was dethroned and exiled. Things were hardly any better in Wessex. There Cynewulf was murdered, and Brihtric was poisoned by his queen. Such scenes as these represent to us the *Niebelungen* as they were acted on the stage of history. And the actors were Christians.

In private life their morals were no better. Though Tacitus extolled the chastity of German women, the respect paid to marriage and to family ties, his praise was merely relative. The Germans entirely lacked the refinement of the old civilizations. On the contrary they were grossly brutal; and under the spur of drunkenness—that terrible form of the vice to which only nations of gloomy temperament are subject—their passions were roused to the verge of madness.

The Penitential ascribed to St. Theodore, which may have been compiled some hundred years after the first converts had been baptized, makes some curious disclosures. In reading through the list of sins, some of them monstrous in their character, one appreciates that in morals these men were still pagans, and that though possessed of higher intelligence they were on the whole little superior to the better races of African negroes. Above all their frequent relapses from the faith no longer give rise to wonder.

They entertained lasting and most bitter hatred. A murder never ended with the death of the victim. In their contracts, their public gatherings, their councils, there was ever question of old alliances being renewed, of reconciliations being made only to yield again to new quarrels. A code of laws existed, but though theft and brigandage were treated severely, murder went almost unpunished. Bands of robbers infested the country, levying blackmail upon the farms, and carrying off the cattle. Though measures were taken to prevent stolen property from being sold, the evil seemed incurable; and all, from highest to lowest, made a practice of pillage.

Slavery formed another feature in the sad picture. Prisoners were offered for public sale, the price of a man being about that of four oxen. Exportation of natives was forbidden, but the thirst for gain was too strong to be restrained by law. Nothing could exceed the barbarity of the men of Bristol, who sent out bands of ruffians to scour the country round and bring in children and women, especially such as were pregnant, to be shipped off to Ireland. This practice lasted until the eleventh century. Only the unceasing energy and continual preaching of Wulfstan, bishop of Worcester, who made journeys across country in pursuit of the traffickers in human flesh, succeeded in the end in killing this long-established pagan tradition.

The fierce and bloody religion of their German forefathers had a share in forming this cruel disposition of the Angles and Saxons. It taught no lesson of meekness and peace. They pictured the thunder god, Thor, the mighty smith, as one who dealt crushing blows with his terrible hammer. If a man died, it was because he had encountered Tiw, the god of the sky, whose symbol was a naked sword. Their chief deity was Woden, the war-God, who from a window of his heavenly palace would gaze out upon the battlefields of men, allotting victory to those he favoured and taking the slain to form his own escort in his passage through the sky. They dreamed of a paradise in which days of carnage should alternate with nights of debauch, when they might drink blood from the skulls of their foes.

Of such a character were the traditions the invaders brought with them from their German home; but after its transplantation to a new soil the old religion had not time to take firm root. Even in Germany before the conquest of Britain it was beginning to lose its hold upon the people. The priesthood, once so powerful, had lost nearly all its influence, and there was no regular worship. Their temples were mere wooden huts enclosing idols in gold, silver or stone, a few symbols of nature, and a table of sacrifice, placed towards the east. Just as every head of a family was his own judge, so was he also his own priest, and himself offered sacrifice to the god of his hearth.

Did the decay of their national religion render easier the task of their conversion? By no means. The faith takes a firmer grip on a race which clings to its errors than on one which believes in nothing at all. It is a paradox of which the truth has been established over and over again in the history of Christianity that old forms of worship which seemed to be perishing under the blight of scepticism are roused into a very delirium of life when brought face to face with the divinely intolerant religion of Christ. So did the coming of the monks to England provoke a reaction towards paganism.

Yet this religious decay seems to have brought with it some advantages. We shall see later how ideas of a superior being, free from the grossness of their native gods, seem to have floated vaguely in the more noble Saxon minds. But a Saxon king was a warrior, and a son of warriors and gods. He breathed hatred with every breath, and regarded vengeance as his natural right. He was not easily led to bow before a God who was born in want and who died in shame, that by the example of His love for man He might teach men to love one another.*

III

IT would be wrong to think, however, that the character of the race was unredeemed by any good qualities. The Anglo-Saxons were manly, as is witnessed by their very vices. They were earnest, as is shown by Ethelbert's answer to Augustine and by Edwin's long deliberations when St. Paulinus first brought him the gospel.

True, this serious bent of their minds easily led to gloominess, and gloom deadens the soul. They were haunted by the thought of death. It pursued them everywhere, running through their songs, and forcing itself into their waking consciousness when they roused themselves from their debauches. But they were used to it, and looked it boldly in the face. The heroes of ancient Greece knew how to fly from death as well as to meet it; no one took it amiss; but the Teuton had to die, and might not fly without dishonour. He rushed to battle with naked breast. Though blows rained upon him, he felt them not. A kind of frenzy added tenfold to his strength; and he laughed as he saw the blood streaming from his wounds.

He could also love; but his love was austere and silent. He was true to his friendships, which were founded on devotion or on his plighted word. He loved his wife deeply and earnestly, though he rarely suffered a smile to give expression to his affection. He loved his lord, and the lord returned the love of his faithful subject,

* Cf. Lavisse, *Études sur l'Hist. d'Allemagne*: La Foi et la morale des Francs.

so that they wept when they parted and dreamed of each other in exile. With them love such as this might become a noble and chivalrous passion.

After the Anglo-Saxons had become Christians, they retained both the faults and the virtues of their race—both its brutishness and its tenderness. Their history is full of strange moral contrasts. One page tells of deeds of brutal violence; another of holy and chivalrous affections told in words which might fitly describe the most passionate human love.

So the Anglo-Saxon race in spite of its ferocity and sensuality possessed many noble qualities which only required the faith to transform them into high moral virtues. It is not true, as is alleged by Taine, that in the first instance temperament and climate alone led them to adopt Christianity; but it is indisputable that only the touch of the gospel was needed to turn those adventurers and robbers into saints; into kings like sweet Oswald of Northumbria, who died on the battlefield crying with his last breath, " O my God, save men's souls;" into apostles like the martyred Boniface; into loving hearts like Bennet Biscop, abbot of Jarrow, who desired to die by the side of his prior Siegfried—himself in the last stages of consumption—and lay down on the same poor couch, his head resting on the same pillow, that he might breathe forth his soul in a last kiss of peace. Little by little love for their crucified Lord was to instil a tender light into their souls and drive thence the gloomy broodings of the Teuton mind. The austere lessons of the Old Testament appealed to them especially; but let us not be unmindful of those "radiant deaths"* of English nuns, who departed amid sounds of heavenly music and a glow of celestial light.

* Montalembert.

Chapter II—ST. GREGORY

I

THE sixth century was drawing to a close. As yet no effort had been made to bring the faith to the Anglo-Saxons. The Church's foreign missions had for the present received a check, for the hordes of Germany had poured down upon the empire. Before attacking the barbarous nations that lay in the rear, the Church must first win to the faith the heretical or pagan forces which were massed within the very territories of Christendom. None of the Churches of the continent might as yet send apostles to the British Isles.

It seemed that those distant shores which Roman conquest had brought for an instant within the ken of civilization, were once more shrouded from view by the thick mists of the northern seas. The islands were well-nigh forgotten. Nothing was known of the bloody revolutions which were raging therein. The historian Procopius looked upon those shores as the mysterious land to which the spirits of the Armoricans sailed after death. From time to time a pilgrim from Wales or from Ireland came over the sea to Italy, and brought back to mind that a Church still lived in those distant parts, orthodox still in spite of a few relics of Pelagianism, in communion still with the centre of unity, but so remote that nothing was known of her uses, while the ordinances of popes and councils never reached her.

Whence then was the faith to dawn upon England? Certainly not from Ireland. Columba, that mysterious apostle of Scotland, had only just founded his monastery on the barren islet of Iona. Already his army of monks had gone forth to battle with paganism in the Highlands, spreading to every island and along the margin of every lake; but time was needed before they might draw into close neighbourhood with the Saxon races. And when at length they were able to preach the gospel and establish the faith in Northumbria, other missionaries had already made their way into the country.

From Wales no help might come. Not that holy men were wanting. David of Menevia lived till A.D. 601; Gildas was writing his Letters from the solitude of his cell; Oudoceus had just replaced St. Teilo in the see of Llandaff. Monks and hermits journeyed from church to church in greater numbers than ever. Synods were held, abuses were put down. Yet the faith never spread beyond the mountain barrier which had withstood the Saxon invader; for war, though not continuous, never ceased to smoulder beneath its own ruins, and constantly burst forth anew: war in the south with the men of Wessex, who won victory after victory under their king Ceawlin; war in the Thames valley with the East Anglians and the growing power of Mercia; war in the north against Ethelfried, king of Northumbria. The long struggle, which bred hate in the mind of the Welsh, and contempt in that of their foes, formed an insurmountable barrier between the two races.

At length in the latter years of the sixth century came the opportunity of Rome. The work of the conversion of the barbarous peoples within her own domain had so far prospered that she had leisure to think of sending missions further afield. A great epoch in her missionary history was about to dawn. Its first-fruits were to be the conversion of the English, to be wrought with St. Augustine as the tool under the guiding hand of St. Gregory the Great.

II

IT was the constant tradition of the Saxon Church that St. Gregory, while abbot of St. Andrew's on the Cœlian Hill, had thought of going forth himself as an apostle to the people of the north. However, Providence, which had led him to resign his office of prætor to become a monk and a saint, would not suffer him to be buried in obscurity among the tribes of Sclavonia or of Germany. Pelagius II. dragged him from his quiet retreat, made him cardinal and sent him to labour for the Church at the court of Constantinople. However fruitful his mission might prove, it was not for a brilliant field such as this that Gregory sighed. His father in religion, St. Benedict, had preached the gospel to the peasants of Monte Cassino, who were in his day still buried in idolatry. St. Placid, the patriarch's dearly beloved disciple, had died a martyr's death in Sicily. Others had been hanged in couples by the Lombards from the trees in the Roman Campagna. The Lateran was crowded with exiles from Monte Cassino, who had fled before the invasion, bearing away in their flight nothing save the book of their rule. St. Gregory felt a holy envy for their lot and saw that he might be better employed than in practising diplomacy at Byzantium.

One day—nothing is known of the date—the abbot of St. Andrew's was passing through the public markets of Rome. Standing amongst the goods which were exposed for sale about the ground were a few bands of slaves. The sight was common enough. At that time slavery was still practised, especially by the Jews, and later on Gregory had a hard struggle with them in defence of the rights of conscience and of liberty. In those days all the Church could do was to temper and refine the rude manners of the age, and to teach to the world the dignity of man, especially of the baptized Christian.

To-day in addition to the usual groups of African negroes and dark-skinned Asiatics or Spaniards that were offered for sale were three youths of remarkable beauty, who had lately arrived from the north. Neither the exposure they had suffered on the journey nor the hot rays of the southern sun had as yet tanned the milky whiteness of their limbs. Their well-cut features, chastened with an air of sadness and crowned with a wealth of fine auburn hair, bore witness to their noble rank, and offered a marked contrast to the care-worn and degraded faces of their companions.

Though St. Gregory had parted with worldly rank, he still preserved a cultivated taste for beauty of form as well as for beauty of language and song. He was something of an artist, and to describe him as an iconoclast shows a gross want of appreciation of the saint's natural character.

He paused, looked at the slaves and enquired whence they came. "They come from Britain," he was told; and to enlarge upon the merits of his wares, the merchant added: "In that island all alike have that clear and beautiful complexion."

"Are they Christians or pagans?" asked the monk.

"Pagans," was the answer.

Gregory sighed. "Alas," he said, "that faces so bright should be the property of the prince of darkness, and that these fair forms should conceal a soul void of God's grace, sick with sin, and ignorant of the bliss of heaven. And what is the name of their race?"

"They are Angles."

Now the saint after the fashion of his day had a taste for word-play.

"Angles? Angels, rather; for they have the faces of angels, and must share with the angels the kingdom of heaven. From what province have you brought them?"

"From Deira."

At that time the English king of Deira, a province which

nearly corresponds with the present counties of York and Durham, had so far taken advantage of the discord which prevailed in the neighbouring kingdom of Bernicia as to possess himself of that territory. In spite of a common origin the Anglo-Saxon tribes regarded each other as foes, and the nobles who became prisoners had no choice save of death or slavery. The young Deirans had doubtless been captured and sold by the enemy, whose defeat left them but little disposed to respect the rights of their fellow-men.

"Deira!" continued the monk. "Aye, *de ira eruti!* From God's ire shall they be snatched, and brought to the mercy of Christ. And what is the name of their prince?"

"Ælla."

"Ælla! Alleluia! Even there shall be sung the praises of God."

So ended that famous dialogue with a word which became like the war-cry of St. German with those who were later to win England for Jesus Christ.

An old chronicler states that Gregory received the captives into his own monastery. The sad spectacle had left a wound in his heart, and more than ever did he dream of going forth to spread the faith in those distant lands.

We are told how he sought out pope Pelagius II., and by dint of entreaty gained permission to go. He knew how well he was loved in Rome; so he set out with all speed and secrecy. A few zealous companions joined him, and these all shared in the secret of his mission. But God had disposed otherwise. For three days had the missionaries continued their journey along the Flaminian Way, when it was discovered at Rome that Gregory was no longer in the city. A crowd hastened to the pope, who at the moment was officiating at the Vatican, and addressed him angrily. "What have you done? You have displeased St. Peter. You have ruined Rome. You have let Gregory leave us. You have driven him out." A riot was imminent.

Meanwhile Gregory and his companions were resting during the heat of the day in a grassy field. Gregory was reading. Suddenly a grasshopper alighted and rested on his book. The saint looked at it for a moment and could not refrain from again making a pun. "*Locusta*," he exclaimed. "An excellent name. It seems to tell us, *Loco sta*, Remain where you are! I see that we shall never reach our journey's end. Let us be moving. Saddle our beasts, and let us start off at once."

At that very moment messengers arrived in hot haste, their horses exhausted and drenched with sweat. They brought an order from Rome that the missionaries should return. Pelagius had yielded with delight to the pressing entreaties of the citizens, and had sent forth the order with all speed.

"You see," said the saint, "it is as I told you. We must return."

So they went back to Rome. This took place before the year 588. In 590 Gregory became pope.

III

NEVER before perhaps had pontiff had to bear so heavy a burden as was now laid upon Gregory's shoulders; and never before had so strong a soul dwelt in a frame so ill adapted from its feebleness to support the load. The times were rough. Gregory had to fight almost at the same moment against patriarchal ambition and imperial tyranny at Byzantium; against schism in Istria; against the Lombards in the plains of the Po; against simony in Gaul; against Arians in Spain and

Donatists in Africa. Italy was reduced to the lowest depths of wretchedness, being the prey of financiers from Greece and of freebooters from Lombardy. Yet Gregory was not content with waging a mere war of defence; he must win new territories to the faith. So he caused the gospel to be preached to the peasants of Corsica and Sardinia, who were still idolaters, and even concerned himself with the spread of the faith in distant Persia.

Gregory's ambitious projects of missionary enterprise must have seemed ill-timed. Men's minds were full of gloomy anticipation, and they thought the end of the world was at hand. The empire was well-nigh crushed beneath its misfortunes, and men imagined that it was about to fall as imperial Rome had fallen before. The city, they thought, would be destroyed, and with her the entire world. Even Gregory was looking out for the last great day when time should resolve into eternity. " Lo ! the world is perishing, towns are razed to the ground, armies are scattered, churches are in ruins ; there is no one to till the soil. And we, a mere handful, all that is left of the people, are ever being struck by the sword which is working our ruin." The city of the emperors, threatened and even besieged by the Lombards, seemed to fulfil the strange prophecies of Ezechiel, and to become as flesh set to boil upon the fire till it is sodden and consumed, or as an eagle in old age shorn of its wings and plumes. "The world is nigh unto its end," he concluded; " let us bury with it our worldly lusts." *

His words might almost convict him of pessimism or of despair. "For eleven months I have scarcely risen from my bed. I have such attacks of gout and such worries that life is a burden to me. I am sinking from very grief. I long for death, the supreme healer. The people and

---

* Ep. iii. 29. Homel. in Ezech.

clergy of this city are suffering from fever. No one has strength left to work. In the country around the dead form the only matter for talk. Death and disease have invaded Africa. In the east matters are still worse. None have escaped. The end of the world is drawing near." *

Yet the pope's energy never wavered. Though his words seem to imply despair, his deeds were those of a man who believed in the future.

IV

THE distant island of the Anglo-Saxons especially engaged his thoughts. The slave-trade still flourished there, and he resolved to make it serve for the salvation of the country which he so much loved. To Candidus, a priest charged with the administration of the little patrimony of St. Peter in Gaul, he wrote as follows:—
"We desire that your charity, with the money which it receives, purchase clothes for the poor; or else young English slaves, from seventeen to eighteen years of age, who shall be devoted to God's service and educated in a monastery. You may thus spend the Gallic coins which have no currency here. . . Since, however, the youths that you may buy in this way will be pagans, I wish a priest to accompany them. If any should happen to fall sick on the journey and be in danger of death, the priest would baptize them. May your charity devote all its zeal to this work."

Were the pope's wishes realized? Many believe that the young slaves were taught in one of the schools in which Gregory himself gave lessons in singing. It is certain that to these schools students flocked both from Gaul and from Germany. However that may be, the pope was unwilling to delay any longer the preaching of the faith in England.

* Ep. ix. 123.

Perhaps his feeble health warned him to act quickly. There was another reason also.

News which reached him from that long forsaken island made him believe that the moment for its conversion had already come. With too great a readiness to regard as actually accomplished that for which he so earnestly longed, he wrote: " We have been informed that the English nation eagerly desires to be converted. But the priests in their neighbourhood "—it is uncertain whether his words refer to the Frankish priests or to the Welsh clergy—" pay no heed to them and do not seek to foster these holy desires by their preaching."

What was the source of this statement, clearly much exaggerated?

In 594 or perhaps early in 595 Gregory of Tours came to Rome, and he may have told the pope that a young Frankish princess who had been left as an orphan to his care, had just wedded an English prince.* The archbishop did not know that prince's name; he did not even know that he was king: "In Cantia regis cuiusdam filius." Naturally then he would know nothing of the motives which had led to the match. In this matter we are better informed than he.

Ethelbert had been king of Kent since his eighth year, and had become somewhat ambitious. He had so often been reminded that as a lineal descendant of Hengest, the invader of Britain, he was by right Bretwalda, or over-lord of the Saxon princes, that he began to find his kingdom too small for him. Yet none possessed so wealthy a domain as he. His neighbours in the Gwent and the Thames valley were continually pressed by war. Kent on the other hand had been conquered long ago, and, cut off as it was by the great forest of Anderida, was developing in peace

* Greg. Tur. 9, 36 sq.

and plenty. A considerable population tilled in security her fair valleys and tree-clad wolds. Her new masters had begun to trade with the continent, and were slowly recovering the maritime power which they had possessed in the past.

Nevertheless the young monarch thirsted for battle and for conquest. In the north-west the Thames barred his progress, as did Anderida in the south-west. There still remained, however, a strip of country round London, where a few Britons long held out. Now London had just fallen, and the Thames valley was free, so Ethelbert rushed in to seize it. A foe whom he little expected to meet joined issue with him near the Kent border in the person of Ceawlin, king of Wessex, whom he believed to be engaged against the Welsh. The Saxon veterans made short work of the Kentish men, who had lost their taste for war. Ethelbert was defeated at Wimbledon, and retired in disgrace. This was in 568, when he was sixteen years of age.

After his rout on the battlefield he sought scope for his ambition in another direction. Before that date, in Justinian's time, the English had taken part in a Frankish embassy to Constantinople. Their presence there had been taken as proof that Britain still formed a portion of the empire.* It is thought that those English legates were sent from Kent; there is no earlier instance on record of relations between Saxon England and a foreign power. The second instance occurred twelve years after Ethelbert's defeat at Wimbledon. The king sought an alliance on the continent, and asked for the hand of a Frankish princess in marriage. About this time Ceawlin, his victor at Wimbledon, was himself routed by the Britons at Faddiley (A.D. 584); the power of Wessex waned, and left a free field to Ethelbert's ambition. Doubtless Gregory of Tours said

* Cf. Procopius, Bel. Goth. iv, 20.

nothing about these by-issues at Rome; but they were to be of considerable importance to England's conversion.

On the other hand the archbishop doubtless had much to tell about the new queen of Kent, Bertha or Adelberga, whose story was a romantic one. She was daughter to Charibert I., king of Paris, and Ingoberga. Her father had been dissolute, like the rest of his family, and had lived in concubinage with mistress after mistress. Amongst others he was attracted by two of the queen's servants, who were daughters to a wool-carder. Ingoberga sought to rescue her lord from his unlawful love by working on his sense of shame. For this purpose she made the wool-carder ply his trade under the palace windows. Charibert became enraged, and straightway wedded one of his two mistresses, giving her the title of queen. Ingoberga was obliged to fly with her child, and Gregory received the two fugitives into his care at Tours. Charibert died excommunicate in 567. In 589 Ingoberga also passed away in a nunnery, leaving Bertha alone in the world. About this time Ethelbert was seeking a Frankish princess for his queen; so they gave him the orphan.

Her guardians had laid down one condition—that Bertha was to be free to practise her faith and to be allowed to have a bishop as chaplain. To this Ethelbert agreed.

Such was the story that Gregory of Tours may have told the pope. He may have added that the king was true to his pledges; that the queen's chaplain was Liudhard, bishop of Senlis; and that the queen had the use of a small but ancient church which had been abandoned since the Saxon conquest.

The church was dedicated to St. Martin, in memory doubtless of the long years which Bertha had spent under the shadow of the great church at Tours. Neither was she unmindful of Radegund, wife of her grandfather, Clotaire I. That holy French queen had died in 587; at this day a street in Canterbury bears her name. Bertha was descended from St. Clotilda, and knew how to pray and to wait. Meanwhile her gentle influence was gradually disposing her superstitious husband to yield to grace whenever God's time should come.

If the pope did not know all these details, at least he knew enough to tell him that it was now time to begin.

Chapter III—ST. AUGUSTINE'S MISSION

I

S T. GREGORY knew where to find his missionaries. To the abbey he was accustomed to look for his trusted agents, and he even wished his palace to be as much like a monastery as it could be made. But more than any other his cherished house of St. Andrew had furnished him at need with bishops, legates, envoys of every kind. Now he required forty monks. He appealed to their kindly affection the more confidently since they knew his design and his longing desire to see it accomplished.

The companions with whom he had started on his own abortive expedition were still there. Gregory's example had fired their zeal, and so forty were found who under the inspiration of God's grace offered themselves for the work. At their head was Augustine, prior of the convent, and with him a priest named Lawrence, who may perhaps have belonged to the secular clergy. We may also mention Peter, the monk, who was to become the first abbot of Canterbury, John, who was also a monk, the little choir-boy Honorius, who afterwards became archbishop, and the deacon James, who to apostolic fervour added a profound love of music. The names of the rest are unknown to us.

At that time the disciples of the pope who had reformed the Church's music were spreading throughout Gaul and Germany.* We see that Gregory did not forget his dear

* Joan. Diac. Vita S. Greg. ii. 8.

English: he doubtless thought that music would open a way into their souls.

Venerable Bede says but little concerning the occupation of Augustine and his companions before they went forth on their mission; he merely tells us that they were monks, filled with the fear of God. The opinion is generally held that they were Benedictines.* They were sprung from the people; for later on the same historian lays stress on the fact that St. Mellitus, the head of a second mission, was a scion of a noble house.

It may seem a little superfluous to say that St. Augustine was of good parts even according to the world's notions. It is, however, as well to make the remark, for the fact has been denied on the simple ground that he was a monk. Of course, the cloister is not a school for worldly wisdom; but ignorance of the world is by no means essential to true religious spirit. So at least Gregory judged, once Roman prætor, now pope of Rome. For his most delicate missions and for those which especially required a knowledge of mankind, he preferred monks. He found that religion and common-sense made up for a good many defects. There were times when he was mistaken, and when his confidence was misplaced, but at least St. Augustine cannot be cited as one of his failures.

Gregory was well acquainted with the prior. He knew him to be docile and enterprising, pious, zealous, and discreet. The fact that Gregory's choice fell upon him is sufficient testimony of his worth and almost renders further information about him unnecessary. Yet the following is the account given by an English Protestant writer.

"In appointing his mission, Gregory was guilty of an error in judgment, attributable in part to the character of the man, and in part, to the spirit of the age. One of

---

* Baronius thinks that they followed the rule of St. Equitius.

the errors of the age was an almost entire forgetfulness of the secondary causes employed in the providence of God; looking always to the First Great Cause, men expected a miraculous interference, and what they expected as a probability they were eager to imagine as a fact. Gregory's notion was, that if he could secure men of vital religion and piety to undertake the mission, the work would be accomplished by the direct interposition of the deity. . . . While all history speaks of the fervent piety, the self-denial, and the consistent moral conduct of the forty missionaries who were sent from Rome, we do not discover amongst them a single man endowed with superior powers of mind, and we find them, in consequence, as a body, defective in moral courage." *

I have selected only one page out of some twenty in the same strain. The writer takes it for granted that only a man of the world can make a successful missionary, and that a mere monk cannot possess ability. Dean Hook's contention shows too much party spirit to need serious consideration. Other Protestant writers show more justice in bearing witness to the high moral courage of the forty missionaries—one of the very virtues which Hook denied them. Thus Kemble, whom Montalembert calls "an author more learned than enthusiastic," compared the departure of those monks to conquer a world at the very time when their own native city was threatened by the Lombards, to the bold action of Scipio in sailing to Carthage when Hannibal was at the very gates of Rome; and the palm of heroism he gave to the monks. M. Lavisse ranks their apostolic enterprise above the victorious expeditions of Agricola. It is true, however, that their heroism was to have its hour of weakness.

* Dean Hook, *Lives of the Archbishops of Canterbury*, vol. i. pp. 49-50.

II

THEY left the holy city about June, A.D. 596, and before long arrived in France. One of their first halting-places in Gaul was the great monastery of Lerins, where St. Patrick had once stayed for nine years. Augustine had to pay a visit on the pope's behalf to Protasius, bishop of Aix, and to the patrician Arigius, a Burgundian of rank. He had to leave his companions at Lerins, and it was doubtless during the absence of their leader on this occasion that, left to themselves, the monks fell into that despondency and discouragement which has become historic. Had they imagined when they gave in their names that their mission was to be free from risk and peril? They knew nothing of the people committed to their charge, and the first account they had of them filled them with dismay.

Certain men, whom St. Gregory vaguely refers to as *maledici homines*, painted the Anglo-Saxons as a race of barbarians, to whom it was vain to attempt to preach the faith. The missionaries would lose their lives; they would not even be allowed to land; moreover they knew not a word of the language; in short their attempt was condemned as an act of madness. Evidence was forthcoming in plenty. The letters of Sidonius Apollinaris, written a century ago, but still looked upon as trustworthy, told of Saxon piracy and slave-raids. There was a dictum of Salvianus, priest of Marseilles, which summed up in a few sentences Roman opinion of the day: " The Goths are treacherous, but modest; the Alans immodest, but frank; the Saxons cruel, but chaste; the Franks liars, but hospitable." They could gauge the character of the Saxons in Britain from that of their continental brethren. Moreover, less than twenty years ago, a band of the latter had separated from the Lombard army and crossed the Alps, plundering, destroying, and enslaving. After having been driven back, they returned with greater numbers, in two armies, this time bringing with them women, children, and cattle. They had seized and consumed on the spot the corn which was standing already cut around Avignon; and, after having purchased the right to cross the Rhone, basely cheated the people of Auvergne by giving bright new brass pieces for gold.

Dismayed by these or similar facts and fancies the missionaries begged leave to return. It must indeed be admitted that something was lacking in the organization of the little army. Reliance may justly have been placed in the saintliness of the monks; but perhaps too little allowance was made for human weakness. Augustine's authority was not strong enough. A simple prior, despite the title of bishop which was to be his if he succeeded in establishing himself a Church, he lacked the power of imposing his own will on his companions. We may well believe that these dispiriting reports had no weight with him; nevertheless he thought well to return to Rome to present the request of his timid brethren. He took with him a small quantity of platters and spoons as a gift from Stephen, abbot of Lerins, to Gregory's poor.

The pope would not listen to the reasons urged for abandoning the mission, and sent Augustine back with a letter addressed to his companions, full of energy and tenderness. "It would have been better not to have undertaken the mission than to draw back after having once set out. Diligently ought you to strive, my dear sons, to bring to a successful issue the task which under grace from the Lord you have undertaken. Let neither hardships on the journey nor evil reports affright you. With all your might and fervour do that to which God has urged you, knowing that the greater your labours the more abundant will be the glory of your everlasting reward. In all humility obey Augustine, your leader, who is returning to you. We have made him your abbot. Be assured that whatever you do in conformity with his directions will tell to the profit of your souls. May God Almighty shield you with His grace and suffer me to see in glory the fruits of your toil; that so, though I am denied a part in your labours, I may be found the associate of your reward; since, had I my wish, I would labour with you. May God take you, my dearest sons, safe into His keeping." *

So the monks had to set out once more under the leadership of their newly-appointed abbot.

III

ST. AUGUSTINE brought other letters with him besides that which we have just quoted. In order to sustain their courage the pope had sketched out the course of their journey. It would prove both long and wearisome, and since the missionaries would not put a blind trust in God's guidance, Gregory took pity on their weakness and made them sure of human help. Then, too, he wished to interest the kings and bishops of Gaul in his undertaking. So he furnished his monks with a letter of recommendation for every royal or episcopal city at which they were likely to stay.

He thanked abbot Stephen and congratulated him on the good order of his house, to which Augustine had borne witness. The patrician Arigius was a devoted servant of the papacy; more than once before had the pope instructed his envoys to do nothing save with his advice. On this occasion he recommended his missionaries to his care. Then there were letters for the bishops. On his journey

* Ep. vi. 15.

Augustine was to act as delegate; he carried the expression of the pope's wishes from town to town, and, at the same time, begged for assistance in his own mission. At Marseilles a portion of the patrimony of St. Peter was in dispute. With the bishop of Arles, Virgilius, the pope was more urgent; no alms had come from his diocese for many years, his predecessor having kept back the moneys which he collected. "It is detestable," he wrote, "that what kings respect, bishops should be said to divert." Then he thanked Protasius, the metropolitan of Aix, for the kindness he had already shown to Augustine, and charged him to see that Virgilius fulfilled his duty, even though he might have to use threats. At Vienne the travellers met Didier, the bishop and future martyr. Thence they travelled to Lyons, and thence on to Autun.

Augustine had now well advanced on his journey to the north, accompanied by his forty monks. In those days travelling from place to place took up a large portion of a bishop's time, and we may suppose that communication was comparatively easy. The network of the Roman roads was still unbroken. There were indeed innumerable taxes to pay, customs, tolls, dues, to say nothing of curious imposts upon carriages, beasts of burden, the grass on which travellers trod, the river banks by which they passed, the dust which they raised. But it is likely that our missionaries were exempt from all these. They went by short stages, making long halts in towns and monasteries. The entire winter of A.D. 596-7 was spent in traversing Gaul. They seem to have stayed a long time at Autun, as a centre, midway between Provence and the north, within easy reach of the royal cities of Metz and Orléans. Bishop Syagrius showed himself so zealous on their behalf that later on the pope sent him the pallium by way of reward. To this very day the bishops of Autun have a right to that distinction in memory of the passage of the apostle.

At this time Brunhild was at the height of her power. The old queen has been a good deal misrepresented. She was tainted with the vices of her race; but those who had known her in her youth, as had Gregory of Tours, recognized in her certain virtues, among them intelligence and even decency. She showed a genuine faith in Christianity. In any case, she had as yet committed none of those crimes which stained her old age; and the pope knew nothing of them up to the time of his death. She was governing in the name of her grandsons the kingdoms of Burgundy and Austrasia. Theodebert reigned at Metz, Theodoric at Châlons and Orléans.

The pope was wont to make Brunhild serve the interests of the Church in France; and if the queen had known how to read between the lines, his letters to her contained a good deal of praise which might have served for advice. He thanked her for her charity, but it was merely a pretext to bring before her notice a thousand abuses, such as simony, idolatry, schism. He sent her certain relics, but only to make her understand that piety must be practical, and for a queen consisted chiefly in protecting the servants of God. "Hasten to appease heaven by chastising the violent, fornicators and robbers, . . . for God might strike you with the whip with which He scourged faithless nations." There is then no need to be astonished that St. Gregory should have asked her to protect his missionaries. He acquainted her with his design and begged her to help them on their way to the English nation. Another letter of similar import was addressed to the two little kings, who must have been still too young to grasp its meaning, for Theodebert was eleven and Theodoric only six; but others might have derived benefit from it.

We do not know what the queen did on Augustine's behalf; but she protected him effectually, and later on received a letter of thanks from the pope.

These letters from St. Gregory are the only authentic documents which relate to Augustine's journey across Gaul. Tradition states that he passed through Angers. From Orléans, where he would have seen Theodoric, the king, he went to Tours, to which St. Martin's tomb doubtless attracted him. Did he dream that the great wonder-worker seemed already to be waiting for him in his little chapel at the threshold of England?

A well known legend is concerned with this part of the journey. In the course of his passage down the valley of the Loire the saint came to Ponts-de-Cé, a spot not very far distant from Angers. The band of missionaries had just crossed the river by the bridge, which was a mile in length, when they found themselves confronted by the villagers, who, seeing the poorly clad strangers approaching on foot, had gathered together and barred the way. Before long the women appeared on the scene. They shrieked like furies and hurled gibes and insults at the strangers. The monks were pursued, pushed hither and thither and even thrown to the ground. They were compelled to fly. There stood near the spot a beautiful leafy elm, beneath which Augustine wished to stop and spend the night; but the women returned again and again to attack them. He had already raised his staff to defend himself against one more violent than the rest, when God intervened. The saint's arm stretched out like a bow, and his staff shot like an arrow to a distance of more than three hundred yards. Followed by his monks, the holy abbot hastened to the spot which God had thus marked. The staff was fixed in the ground, and a beautiful spring had gushed forth. They quenched their thirst, and giving thanks to God, spent the night in holy song. And lo! in the neighbouring village the people saw streams of light fall from heaven and rest above the missionaries. Then they recognized their fault.

Meanwhile the night drew to a close. At dawn the

people of Cé hurried to the spot; but they were too late, for their victims of the day before were already far on their way to Angers. Then they grieved for their sin the more that the miraculous spring told them of the blessings they had lost. Looking on the ground they saw written in the sand: "Here rested the servant of the servants of God, Augustine, sent by the most blessed pope Gregory for the conversion of the English."

They determined to build a church over the place, and marvellously it came about that no woman might either enter the church or drink at the spring. So that pilgrims from Angers, who went in great numbers to Canterbury, were amazed that women might freely enter the saint's church; it showed, they said, that the Saxon women were more charitable than those of Angers. Now a well-known lady from the neighbourhood of Angers sought one day to put this strange prohibition to the proof. Holding in her hand a large wax taper, as though to appease the saint, she tried to cross the threshold. An invisible force threw her to the ground, and she expired, her bowels bursting open. Then they understood the awful lesson.

However, that women might not be absolutely deprived of the favours of St. Augustine, there was built just outside the door a little recess where they might pray and assist at mass. *

A bishop of Angers, named Geoffrey, went on a pilgrimage to Canterbury in the time of Goscelin, the hagiographer. After having shown that the traditions of the two Churches were alike, he narrated a miracle of which he said he had been an eyewitness. Devotion towards the saint had spread through Anjou, especially since the

* Similar legends were common in the middle ages. One of the most famous is that which attaches to Durham cathedral, where the Galilee was built to accommodate the women whom St. Cuthbert would not suffer to approach his shrine in the church itself.

Norman conquest had brought about more frequent intercourse between England and France. The little expiatory church of Ponts-de-Cé was enlarged, and the bishop came for the consecration. It was May 26, the saint's feast-day. The fields were beautiful with the growing corn. A large crowd gathered for the ceremony, and grew in numbers till the highways were thronged. Then the people crossed over the hedges to where the crops were growing, and in a short time trampled them under foot. A whole year's toil seemed lost. However, prayers were offered to the saint, and ere a month had gone by, the crops grew green again, rose high above the ground, and surpassed in the harvest the people's utmost hopes. And so, says the historian, the new miracle confirmed the old.*

In the spring of 597 the band of missionaries, accompanied with a few interpreters, at length left the shores of France. If, as is probable, they sailed from Boulogne, they must before long have caught sight of the cliffs of Dover, fretted by the sea, and standing out like lofty white walls.

As the fleet bearing the Roman legions had done long years before, the ship doubled the cape, where formerly a great beacon burned from a tower to serve as a lighthouse. Then the coast-line sank lower and lower: the chalky cliffs ran inland, their round summits crowned with green woods and grassland. A long stretch of sand curved like a scythe towards the north, bordered by a Roman road. The cliff appeared again on the horizon, making a white framework to the pretty bay, in which the flat-bottomed vessels of the Saxons had replaced the guard-ships of the Roman fleet.

The ship still kept on her course. On the left between the coast and the triangular isle of Thanet, the sea

* Goscelin, Vita S. Aug.

branched out into a channel of considerable width, dotted with little sandy islets. The entrance was commanded by a low promontory, crowned by a square fort with thick embattled walls, and armed with a tower at each corner. On its slopes lay a deserted town with red-roofed Roman houses, decaying and desolate, an amphitheatre, and at the foot the ruins of a quay. This was the Rutupiæ of the Romans, afterwards Richborough—a town celebrated in its day; the centre of a long chain of fortified places, which stretched the whole length of the coast; the starting-place of all the Roman roads in Britain; a great trading port, from which cargoes of wheat were shipped to Rome; a shore famous for its small but delicate oysters, so esteemed even in the markets of the capital. But for the last hundred years Rutupiæ had lain deserted and in ruins.

The vessel put into shore at a little harbour in the isle of Thanet.* As soon as Augustine had landed, he sent a message to king Ethelbert. He told him how he had come from Rome the bearer of good tidings, promising to whosoever would hearken the everlasting joys of heaven and a kingdom without end with the living and true God.

Whilst awaiting the messenger's return the monks had a few days in which to acquaint themselves with the barbarians who had so terrified them from a distance. They met the common-people clad in smocks of woollen cloth or coarse linen, with tight sleeves delicately embroidered at the shoulders and breast. Their legs were swathed with parti-coloured bands, and a hood covered their heads. The

* Ebbsfleet has been generally accepted of late years as the site of the landing, but the distinguished geologist Professor McKenny Hughes, in a sensible little essay appended to Canon Mason's *Mission of St. Augustine* (1897), pronounces in favour of Richborough itself. "The only positive evidence," he says, "which we possess is in favour of the belief that Augustine's first night in England was spent beneath the rock-like walls of the Roman fortress of Richborough."

chieftains wore in addition a cross-belt, a sword with gilded hilt, and a short blue cloak covered with fanciful embroidery. The monks doubtless entered the wooden Saxon huts and the huge halls, where after supper the men, seated around on benches, drank beer, served by the women, whilst the harp passed from hand to hand, and a poet sang or a jester cut his capers. Perhaps hospitality compelled the strangers to sleep there, on trusses of straw, in an atmosphere of smoke, with their feet to the fire, which blazed in the centre of the hall : a foretaste of missionary life.

Ethelbert's reply was not long in coming. The king ordered the strangers to remain in Thanet; he himself would come to see them. At the same time he gave orders that they should want for nothing. *

Ethelbert was hesitating. He knew something of Christianity from his queen and bishop Liudhard. Both had been quietly preparing the way for the gospel—perhaps a little timidly, for St. Gregory seems later on somewhat to reproach queen Bertha with having been behindhand in the matter of her husband's conversion. Whilst he was still offering sacrifices to his gods in an old Roman building, Bertha and Liudhard only a few steps away would be praying and singing God's praises in the little church of St. Martin. They had preached by example, and without uttering a word about religion had softened the king's heart. But Liudhard was now dead, and the queen remained the only Christian in the country. St. Augustine's arrival was timed not a moment too soon. The king had the vague ideas of a barbarian about religion; he thought it a kind of magic. If he did not make up his mind

---

* According to a local tradition queen Bertha came to see the missionaries whom God had sent her. In the church at Minster is shown the stone on which Augustine is said to have seated himself during the interview.

at once, it was because he was afraid of those men who had come from so far. He was afraid of their charms, and, feeling sure that he had nothing to fear in the open air, he at first forbade them to enter Canterbury, being resolved to go and meet them himself. Might we not almost fancy ourselves to be reading some story of our present-day missions, where zeal has so often to overcome the childish mistrust and suspicion of some petty savage prince?

On the day named the king went to Thanet and summoned the strangers to a conference. He took his seat under a tree surrounded by his warriors. All were armed, and carried a lance or sword in the hand, a helmet of ironwork shaped like the head of a wild-boar, a coat of mail, and on the arm a wooden buckler with an iron boss. Meanwhile the monks formed themselves into procession. A massive silver cross was carried at their head, and behind it a large gilt panel bearing upon it a painted figure of our Saviour. Then came the body of monks, and lastly Augustine himself, who towered head and shoulders above the rest. They were singing the litanies, and for the first time Gregorian melodies were heard in England, where for a thousand years afterwards they were to fill the vaulted arches of countless monastic churches. The Saxons gathered at the meeting-place must have been struck by that sweet and solemn chant sung in alternate choirs, and so little like their own German hymns; but they could not appreciate the solemnity of the scene, unique in the history of the Church, at which the old barbarian world, represented by the king and his subjects seated on the grass, awaited the advent of the truth borne towards them in song.

In other countries the faith had glided in secretly. It had fallen like a seed on the idolatrous soil, brought over, no one knows how, by that tide of trade and war which commingles men and ideas. It had grown slowly, until, when men strove by repeated blows to cut it down or to uproot it from the soil, it was found to have become a strong and great tree. Here there was nothing of the kind. In the open air, on a plain strewn with ruins, amidst the débris of a highly developed civilization, by the side of the rough and sullen sea which had brought to their shores in turn both Cæsar's galleys and the barks of their fathers, the Saxons stood in silence, a little mistrustful of this third invasion. The procession slowly advanced along the beach, singing strange but peaceful melodies. Clad in their monkish habit, those forty conquerors brought blessings of which the barbarians had no suspicion—civilization, new arts, literature, a bond with the old world, an intense spiritual life, germs of saintliness which in the next generation were to blossom forth, and ten centuries of religious splendour. The Christian history of England was about to begin, and what a beautiful tale it was to unfold!

The king watched the monks' approach. When they were quite near, he made a sign to them to sit down. Then St. Augustine is said to have addressed them through an interpreter to the following effect:

"Your everlasting peace, O king, and that of your kingdom, is the object we desire to promote in coming hither; we bring you, as we have already made known, tidings of never-ending joy. If you receive them, you will be blessed for ever, both here and in the kingdom which is without end. The Creator and Redeemer of the world has opened to mankind the kingdom of heaven, and of citizens of the earth makes men inhabitants of a celestial city. For God so loved the world that He gave His only-begotten Son for the world, even as that only-begotten testifies, that all who believe in Him should not perish but have everlasting life. For with so boundless a love did the same Son of God love the world, His creatures, as not only to become man among men, but to deign to suffer death for men, even the death of the cross. For so pleased it His unspeakable clemency to bruise the devil, not in the majesty of His own Divine Nature, but in the weakness of our flesh, and so to snatch us, the worthy prey of the evil one, by the unworthy punishment of the cross, from the jaws of that most wicked prince. Whose Incarnate Deity was manifested by innumerable displays of power, by the healing of all diseases, and the performance of all virtues. He showed Himself God and Lord over the sky, stars, earth, sea, and hell. He calmed by His authority the winds and the sea; He trod the waves of the sea, as though they had been a solid plain; at length, deigning as man to die for men, on the third day He rose from the dead as God; and, by His effulgence, adorned with brighter light the sun, which had been darkened at the death of its Creator. He rose, I say, that He might raise us; He ascended into the heavens, that He might gather us together there in triumph. From thence He shall come as judge of all the world, that He may place believers in His Kingdom, and condemn unbelievers for ever. Do not, therefore, most illustrious king, regard us as superstitious, because we have been at pains to come from Rome to your dominions for the sake of your salvation and that of your subjects, and to force upon an unknown people benefits, as it were, against their will. Be assured, most loving king, that we have purposed this, constrained by the necessity of great love. For we long, beyond all the desires and glory of the world, to have as many fellow-citizens with us as we can in the kingdom of our God; and we strive with all our efforts to prevent those from perishing who may be advanced to the company of the holy angels. For this goodwill the lovingkindness of our Christ has everywhere infused, by the inestimable sweetness of His Spirit, into all the preachers of His truth, that, laying aside the thought of their own necessities, they burn with zeal for the salvation of all nations, and esteem every people as their parents and sons, their brethren and kinsmen; and, embracing all in the single love of God, labour to bring them to everlasting ages of all happiness and festal joys. Such men as these, standard-bearers of our King, made witnesses of God by numberless miracles, through swords, through fires, through beasts, through every kind of torment and death, have with unconquered courage subdued the world to their Saviour. Long since has Rome, long since has Greece, with the kings and princes of the earth, and isles of the gentiles, drawn by the invitations of these preachers, with all the world, rejoiced to worship the Lord of kings and to serve Him for ever, by whom and with whom they may reign eternally. Moved, too, by such love as this, Gregory, the present Father of all Christendom, thirsting most ardently for your salvation, would have come to you, hindered by no fear of punishment or death, had he been able (as he is not) to leave the care of so many souls committed to his charge. And therefore he has sent us in his place to open to you the way of everlasting life and the gate of the kingdom of Heaven; in which, if despising the idols of devils, you refuse not to enter through Christ, you shall most assuredly reign for ever." *

When he had finished, Ethelbert made a reply which Montalembert describes as "loyal, frank, and, in the language of to-day, truly liberal."

* This discourse is given, from tradition apparently, or pious conjecture, rather than documentary authority, in Goscelin's Life. (Bollandists, May 26.) The translation here given is taken from F. Oakeley's *St. Augustine* in the Tractarian "Lives of English Saints."

"Fair, truly, are the words and promises which you bring me, but they are new to me and of doubtful authority. I cannot, therefore, accept them, to the neglect of those religious observances to which, in common with the whole English people, I have so long adhered. However, you are foreigners, who have come a long way to my country, and, so far as I find myself able to understand the object of your visit, you are come with the desire of imparting to me what you yourselves believe to be true and excellent. We are far, then, from wishing to molest you; rather we would receive you with kindness and hospitality. We shall, accordingly, take measures for supplying you with all necessary articles of food. Neither do we forbid you to preach, and make what converts you can to the faith of your religion." *

Ethelbert's speech was like a charter of religious liberty couched in terms of quiet common-sense. Enthusiasm has sometimes made converts. In the story of what followed the battle of Tolbiac is an epic force which stirs one's blood. Even though popular fancy have added to it—I do not deny that it has,—it still shows what were the ideals of our forefathers. But there is not the least trace of romancing in the narrative of Venerable Bede. The king and his followers examined, weighed and pondered, and an English Protestant historian could say without too much flattering his fellow-countrymen:

"Such an answer, simple as it was, really seems to contain the seeds of all that is excellent in the English character—exactly what a king should have said on such an occasion—exactly what, under the influence of Christianity, has grown up into all our best institutions. There is the natural dislike to change, which Englishmen still retain; there is the willingness at the same time to listen

---

* Bede, i 25; F. Oakeley, *St. Augustine*, p. 99.

favourably to anything which comes recommended by the energy and self-devotion of those who urge it ; there is, lastly, the spirit of moderation and toleration, and the desire to see fair play, which is one of our best gifts, and which, I hope, we shall never lose. We may, indeed, well be thankful, not only that we had an Augustine to convert us, but that we had an Ethelbert for our king." *

The Kentish warriors assented to the speech of their chieftain, according to their custom, by shouting "Aye, aye," and by clashing their weapons on their shields. They then dispersed.

V

SOON afterwards, at the king's invitation, the monks quitted the isle of Thanet, passed through the ruins of Richborough, and took the Roman road towards Canterbury.

The spot upon which they had remained during those few days was afterwards held as sacred. Legends grew up around it. The missionaries' sojourn there, it was said, had given fertility to the soil; neither rats nor snakes were found there; Thanet became an earthly paradise, a holy isle. The rock on which Augustine planted his foot on landing received and preserved the impression of that first step of his on English soil The stone which bore that miraculous imprint always kept in its place, and persisted in returning to the beach whatever attempts were made to remove it. A chapel was built there, but this has long since disappeared, and a small farm now stands in its place. A slight ridge of soil rising above the surrounding plain is all that remains of the beach where the power of Rome landed in Britain for the second time.

* Dean Stanley, *Memorials of Canterbury*, p. 34

The neighbourhood of Richborough also has its legend, which in olden days was consecrated by the presence of a hermitage and of a little parish church. A sort of cruciform swelling, not easy to account for, on which the short grass shows distinctly amid the surrounding wheat, was called so lately as last century the Cross of St. Augustine. It was said to mark his track across the ruins.* The neighbourhood has been much changed by the passage of time. The cliffs have been eaten away by the sea, the sea in turn has been forced to retire by the encroaching mud of the Stour. Gaps have been filled up and outlines have become modified and softened. Since the time of Venerable Bede the Wantsome or Thanet Channel has been gradually dwindling. In the sixteenth century a fairly large ship might yet have ventured there at high tide. But to-day all that remains is a narrow ditch filled with rushes lying across a low plain. Richborough lies far inland, and the sea has receded a league. From the solitary hill on which the ruins stand the eye gazes over miles of sand-hills, marsh-land, and gardens. No more peaceful sight can be imagined than that offered by the stretch of country there shut in between the wooded slopes of Thanet, the Ramsgate cliffs so gaily crowned by the pretty town, and the sea ever so sad and grey.

That small spot of land lying just opposite the continent is eloquent with history. It was for long the gateway to the Englishman's island home. On the south, at Deal, landed Cæsar with his Romans; at Ebbsfleet, in Thanet, the Saxons leaped ashore; from the same place a century and a half later St. Augustine and his monks set out in procession to Canterbury to win seven kingdoms to Christ. From that spot, therefore, our island received its early civilization, the primitive elements of its race and its

* In the theory of Professor McKenny Hughes this cross marks the site of the chapel built near St. Augustine's landing-place.

ancient faith. The Romans have left us a few crumbling walls at Richborough; the Saxons their burial-places. But the whole country round tells of the monks who brought the faith. Villages, hamlets, manors, almost everything, before the Reformation belonged to the two monasteries of Canterbury. It seemed only their due. The land was theirs as far as the convent of Minster, where formerly dwelt sweet St. Mildred, *virgo nardiflua*. Over the little arm of the sea which separated Thanet from the mainland the lay brethren plied the ferry. Further down the monks won the foreshore from the waves foot by foot, and a bank there still bears the name of *the Monks' Wall*.

Within recent times religious houses have again sprung up around the spot, as though to purify the soil polluted by three centuries of heresy; and from a tower on the top of the Ramsgate cliffs there sometimes floats, as though prophetic of days to come, a blue and white flag embroidered with the pallium of St. Augustine and the Benedictine motto *Pax*. *

---

* The Benedictines have at Ramsgate an abbey, college and mission dedicated to St. Augustine.

Chapter IV—CANTERBURY

I

AFTER having proceeded for seven or eight hours along the top of the hills which overlook the valley of the Stour, Augustine came in sight of Canterbury. Lying among the trees at his feet he must have seen a large straggling village, amongst the cottages of which arose here and there both Roman houses and British tumuli. Half-way down the hill stood the little church of St. Martin; behind it flowed the Stour, in those days an important stream.

The Canterbury of to-day with its twenty thousand inhabitants is a small provincial town, dull and somewhat sleepy. It is scarcely any bigger now than during the Norman period, yet it is the most ancient of our Saxon towns. In other parts of the country the English dwelt in scattered homesteads or else in small villages; but the Kentish men, being more advanced in civilization and more peaceful in disposition, already possessed the germ of a city. The Roman walls were still standing and served for a boundary. The lines of the old streets, however, were concealed beneath thick layers of rubbish. Over them the Saxons built their huts on the surface of the ground without any foundations. As these increased in number they formed irregular streets; and thus grew up the little capital which under the hand of Providence was destined to be the cradle of the faith in England.

Before entering the city the monks again formed in procession, headed by the silver cross and the picture of our Lord. The day was the 25th of April. In Rome the Greater Litanies were being sung,* and holy relics were borne through the streets in procession from shrine to shrine amid the singing of prayers and anthems. The Church prayed God to bless the fruits of the earth and to ward off all peril. Augustine was unwilling to forego that great liturgical function of the Roman Church; so the youngest of his company, St. Gregory's choir-boy Honorius, intoned the prayers for the day. The procession entered the city at the moment they were singing the words, "We beseech Thee, O Lord, in Thy mercy to vent not Thine anger and Thy wrath on this city and Thy holy house, for we have sinned. Alleluia." †

Being as yet undecided what course to take, Ethelbert offered the strangers a temporary resting-place at a spot called Stable Gate.‡ This was beyond the city walls, close to the Roman buildings which served the king for a palace. St. Martin's they used as their church. "From the time they took possession of their new dwelling," writes Venerable Bede, "they sought to put in practice the apostolic life of the early Church by means of incessant prayer, watchings and fastings. They preached the word of life to whomsoever they might. They despised the

* It is generally supposed that the Greater Litanies were only instituted by St. Gregory in the year 598, and therefore at an epoch later than St. Augustine's coming to England; but it is at least probable that St. Gregory only gave shape and permanence to an earlier Christian custom which had grown out of the processions of the pagan Robigalia.

† This antiphon is found in a MS. of the Church of Lyons amongst those sung at the end of the Litanies on the second day of the Rogations. It may possibly have come from Vienne, where the Rogation processions were first instituted. In the *Ampleforth Journal*, April, 1897, may be found a transcription of the music to which it was sung, from a MS. of the twelfth century.

‡ Father Morris, who knew Old Canterbury well, calls the spot Staplegate—"evidently from the *Staple* or market outside the new Northern Gate." (*Canterbury: Our Old Metropolis*, p. 7.)

things of this world as though they knew them not, only accepting from their disciples what was needful for their support. They put in practice what they taught. They were ready to suffer persecution and even death for the truth which they preached."

God had given new courage to those timid souls. They had gradually mastered the rude and primitive language which had before filled them with such misgivings. We are not told that God gave them the gift of tongues, but other miracles were worked at their hands. "They healed the sick and suffering that were brought to them, or whom they visited," says Goscelin. "There were none, or only very few of Augustine's companions who had not the gift of healing." *

Before long their labours began to bear fruit. The inhabitants, marvelling at their simple and spotless lives and the heavenly sweetness of their teaching, believed and begged to be baptized. Ethelbert did not hold back long, for before the paschal season had expired he also declared himself a believer. Bede sums up the history of these conversions in a very few words: "He and many others, won by the pure lives and by the sweet promises of those holy men, believed and were baptized." That is all he says. That great event, which both for religious and political importance might well vie with the conversion of Clovis, never took hold of popular fancy, and is remembered only in a very few and very meagre local traditions.

The baptism would have taken place at Whitsuntide. We know nothing of the instruction and preparation which the royal catechumen and his fellow converts received. According to Goscelin Ethelbert, "abasing his royalty, sought to throw himself at the feet of the servant

* The Life of St. Augustine by Goscelin, a monk of the eleventh century, is of course quite uncritical. He can only be quoted as having given shape to certain vague legends which existed in his time.

of Christ, by whom he was to be born again. The minister of salvation received him with fatherly tenderness, and exhorted him to wipe out his past sins by abstinence, forgiveness, almsgiving, tears, and other pious works. . . . Then Ethelbert forgives all men that he may be forgiven; by temporal works of mercy he makes himself fit for blessings from on high. The prison doors are thrown open; chains are loosed, captives are set free; the poor and the prisoners eat side by side with the king's friends."

At the appointed time, probably on the Saturday night before Whit-Sunday, the ceremony took place in St. Martin's church. An immense crowd gathered from all parts of Kent and even neighbouring kingdoms to witness the strange sight of a son of Woden renouncing the worship of his fathers. The monks had adorned the little church and especially the font to the best of their power. The display must have been rude enough; but never before perhaps had the prayers appointed for that day been so well fitted to the occasion.

"O Lord, who dost continually increase Thy Church by the calling of the Gentiles, vouchsafe ever to extend Thy protection over those whom Thou art about to cleanse in the waters of baptism. . . . Do Thou, who bringest together divers nations in the praise of Thy name, grant us the will and the power to do what Thou commandest, that this people whom Thou hast summoned to Thine everlasting kingdom, may be one in faith and Thy loving service."

So, we may believe, Augustine prayed, and then he blessed the water according to the use of Rome. First he sang that long preface to the grave and solemn melody we know so well, but which must have sounded so strange to Saxon ears. "I bless thee, creature of God, by Jesus Christ, His only Son, our Lord, . . . who gave thee forth with blood from His side; who commanded His disciples to wash in thee those who should believe, saying: Go teach ye all nations, baptizing them in the name of the Father, and of the Son, and of the Holy Ghost."

Then the baptism began. The royal catechumen and the rest put off their garments and advanced to the font. Augustine asked them the following questions :

" Do you believe in God the Father Almighty ?

" Do you believe also in Jesus Christ, His only Son, our Lord, who was born and suffered ?

"' Do you believe also in the Holy Ghost, in Holy Church, in the remission of sins, in the resurrection of the flesh ? "

" I do believe," answered Ethelbert; and he stepped into the basin of the font, where the priest thrice poured water upon his head, while repeating the sacramental words.

Then the others came forward each in turn. Meanwhile the choir of monks chanted the litanies, repeating each invocation first seven times, then five times, then thrice, for the catechumens were very many. After all were baptized, Augustine sang mass, at which Ethelbert was present, clad in a white robe. At the mass he made his first communion, and afterwards partook of water, milk and honey, which had first been blessed by the priest.

The holy day of Pentecost was dawning ere the long ceremony was ended ; and with it dawned the faith in England.

III

A NEW Church had been founded, and the gospel quickly spread through Kent. The king's example no doubt drew many of his subjects to Christ, but their choice was left free. "Though the king rejoiced at their conversion to the faith," wrote Bede, " he would compel no man. But those that believed he embraced with the greater affection as being his fellow citizens of the heavenly kingdom. For he had learnt from the teachers to whom he owed salvation, that Christ's service must be free and unconstrained." *

St. Martin's was soon found to be too small, and it was necessary to build a larger church. The king made two important gifts of land to provide for the Church's future needs. No doubt the Saxon nobles too had a share in this generous deed; for the king might not appropriate any part either of the folkland or of the crown-land without consent of the *witenagemot* or council of state. He only had the free disposal of his own goods.

First the monks needed a dwelling. At the foot of the hill on which St. Martin's stands, between the church and the city, was a stretch of waste land. There stood upon it an ancient building dating from the Roman occupation, shaped like a basilica. This had served Ethelbert as a temple for his idols. The ground was given to Augustine, and the monks at once set to work to build a convent, which afterwards became the abbey of SS. Peter and Paul. It was the first landed property acquired by the Church of England, whose vast possessions in the middle ages made her the wealthiest of the Churches in the west.

By this time the summer of A.D. 597 was drawing to a close. The new-born Church had thrived; and it seemed time that Augustine should receive consecration as bishop in accordance with the pope's instructions. So he left his companions to continue preaching the faith in Kent, while he himself set out for Gaul. His journey was soon accomplished. By November 16 he had reached Arles, where he was consecrated by Virgilius, archbishop of that city.

Why did Augustine travel so far as Arles for consecration, when he might have received it from prelates much nearer at hand? The pope had so arranged the better to signify the dependence of the new Church on the Holy See.

* Bede, ii. 26.

Rome was too far distant; but the archbishop of Arles had precedence of the metropolitans of France. His Church was regarded as the fountain-head whence the faith had flowed into the other provinces of Gaul; and for this reason he held the rank of legate of the Holy See.* It was from Rome then that Augustine sought his bishopric; and it was Rome who gave him consecration.

A little later, after Augustine had returned to his flock, St. Gregory wrote as follows to his friend Eulogius, patriarch of Alexandria: "Since you not only do good yourself, but share in the gladness of others, I return your favour with news not unlike your own. For the nation of the Angles, who are situated in a far corner (*angulo*) of the world, have been up to this time unbelievers, worshipping stocks and stones; but by the help of your prayers I resolved that, obedient to God's inspiration, I ought to send a monk from my own monastery to them to preach. By my authority (*licentia a me data*) he was made bishop by the bishops of Germany,† and with their assistance reached that nation at the world's end. Now letters have reached us telling of his safety and of his work, that he and those who were sent with him shine amongst that people with such miracles that they seem to rival the powers of the apostles in the signs which they show. And on the feast of our Lord's birth, occurring in this first indiction, we are informed that more than ten thousand English were baptized by this our brother and fellow bishop. I tell you this that you may be made aware what you are doing by your prayers at the very limits of the world as well as by your words among the people of Alexandria. For your prayers

---

* S. Greg. Epist. v. 53.

† At this period the name Germania was not unfrequently applied to any part of Gaul which was under Frankish rule. Cf. Sidon. Apollin., "Lugdunensis Germania."

are at a place where you are not, even as your holy works are manifested where you are." *

With very great rejoicing must the newly consecrated bishop have been hailed on his return to English soil; for "more than ten thousand English" were ready for baptism. Christmas day saw them gathered on the banks of the Swale, a little inlet of the sea which cuts off the swampy isle of Sheppey from the mainland of Kent. †

For lack of historical information we must fall back upon the legends which have come down to us regarding some of the miracles worked by our saint or his companions, and referred to in general terms in Gregory's letter. Augustine was once walking out of doors with his monks, heedless of the bitter weather. The crowd that gathered round them kept increasing at every step. They met by the roadside a beggar, who was both blind and stricken with palsy. The poor fellow had been told that he who was passing by was a bishop and head of the Christians, and cried out, "Augustine, of thy great bounty, help me." The bishop stopped, and, like Peter in the Temple, said to him, "Silver or gold I have none, but what I have I give to thee: arise and be healed in the name of our Lord Jesus Christ." The beggar rose up with his sight restored and with the use of his limbs; then he followed the saint and went like the rest to be baptized.

Now the crowd was very great. There were ten thousand men, says Goscelin, to say nothing of women and children. On account of their numbers it was necessary that the ceremony should take place quickly. So all entered the water, which in spite of its depth gave them a firm footing.

* Ep. viii. 30.

† Not the Yorkshire Swale, as stated by Goscelin, who confounds the conversions made by Augustine with those of St. Paulinus in Northumbria.

There, by direction of St. Augustine and the monks, they baptized one another two and two. When they came back to the bank, it was found that many sick persons had been healed.

V

MEANWHILE the Church of Canterbury was gradually taking organized shape. The monks had built their convent on the land given them by the king. The buildings were rough and simple, for the abbeys of those days bore but little likeness to the magnificent structures of later times, which lacked nothing that might tend to the better observance of religious life in the cloister. Deserted villas and other ruined remains of the old Roman city, as well as log-huts and even caves, were made to serve the purposes of the monastery. At Canterbury the monks turned architects and taught the Saxons some of the secrets of the trade; for example, they showed them how to make the famous Roman mortar, so that in examining the remains of old buildings which were restored at that period, it is sometimes difficult to tell at a glance which portions really date from Roman times.

It was the design of the king and his apostle that the monastery they were building first should serve as a burial-place for the king's family and for the bishops of Canterbury. For that reason it was set up beyond the city walls, beside a road already lined with ancient tombs. Augustine, queen Bertha, Ethelbert, were all buried there after their deaths. In later years other kings also were laid there, as well as six archbishops and no less than seventy abbots.

Augustine was anxious that his cathedral city should remind him of the Rome he loved so dearly; for Rome was the cradle of his own religious life, as well as the source and fountain-head whence England drew the faith. So the convent church, of which the first stone was laid in 598, was dedicated to the apostles SS. Peter and Paul. It became the Vatican of the English Rome.

The little pagan temple which stood within the precincts of the new monastery was made into a chapel. The bishop purged it from the pollution of idolatry; and the altar at which Ethelbert had been wont to offer sacrifice to stocks and stones instead of being demolished was consecrated to the true God. Legends tell us that, when first Augustine offered the holy sacrifice at the spot, Satan, enraged at being thus ousted from his domain, strove to bring down the walls about his enemies' heads. The walls would not yield; but the devil's claws penetrated deep into the masonry. Thorn, the chronicler, speaks of marks to be seen, even in his time, which were accounted as "marks of the beast."

The chapel was dedicated to St. Pancras—further testimony to Augustine's tenderness for Rome and his affection for the pope, for Gregory dearly loved the boy-martyr, and had sought to restore devotion to him in the eternal city. That devotion he perhaps deemed a kind of heirloom, for the martyr had dwelt on the Cœlian Hill at the spot where there stood in after years Gregory's own paternal mansion and his monastery of St. Andrew. *

Besides the three chapels and churches already built, St. Martin's, St. Pancras' and the Holy Apostles, a cathedral church was still needed. Ethelbert gave generously to the foundation; he even surrendered his own palace for the purpose together with the grounds in which it stood. Once

* On the Cœlian also was built the church of the *Quatuor Coronati*, but a few yards distant from St. Andrew's. There Augustine must often have worshipped, and devotion to these saints also took root at Canterbury, in which city once existed a parish dedicated in their honour.

more St. Augustine built upon the ruins of British Christianity, for an ancient church, which had been spared at the conquest, was restored and became the metropolitan church. It was dedicated "to our God and Saviour, Jesus Christ," in memory of the church of our Saviour at the Lateran. Later it became known as Christchurch.

Like most of the Saxons the king cared little for the confinement of city life, so he withdrew to Reculver, an ancient Roman fortress on the north coast, which once guarded both the Wantsome and the approach to the Thames.

"If the baptism of Ethelbert," wrote Dean Stanley, "may in some measure be compared to the baptism of Constantine, so this may be compared to that hardly less celebrated act of the same emperor (made up of some truth and more fable)—his donation of the "States of the Church," or, at least, of the Lateran Palace, to pope Sylvester; his own retirement to Constantinople in consequence of this resignation. It is possible that Ethelbert may have been in some measure influenced in his step by what he may have heard of this story. His wooden palace was to him what the Lateran was to Constantine; Augustine was his Sylvester; Reculver his Byzantium." *

St. Gregory carried the parallel further by telling queen Bertha that she was the Helen of the new Constantine. And so Canterbury became a Rome in miniature. "The English Church," says the Abbé Duchesne, "was a daughter of the great Roman Church; a daughter born out of due time, but perhaps better loved, and certainly more like her mother and more closely fostered beneath her mother's wing, than were her elder sisters." †

---

* *Memorials of Canterbury*, p. 39. † *Églises Séparées*, p. 5.

VI

WE can form a fairly accurate picture of what St. Augustine's cathedral was like. It was destroyed, with all the manuscripts and charters it contained, by the great fire of 1067, when the entire city fell a prey to the flames. So thorough was the destruction that when Lanfranc came three years later he had to receive consecration in a shed. Up to the date mentioned the church, though often restored, seems to have kept to its original plan. Eadmer the historian, a friend of St. Anselm, had frequented it in his boyhood as a chorister, and used to sing there with the Saxon monks. Later on he himself became a monk in the same monastery after it had been rebuilt and reconstituted with a Norman community. Owing to his intimacy with St. Anselm he shared that great archbishop's exile and followed his dear master to Rome. There, when he visited the ancient church of the Vatican, he was struck by its astonishing resemblance to the former cathedral of Canterbury. Of course the Roman church was much longer and wider, and far more richly adorned with glittering mosaics and marbles. But it was a basilica of the same type, with its tall nave running down the middle; its altar rising beneath a circular apse; its crypt, which opened between the two rows of steps leading up to the *presbyterium*; and its choir for monks and canons at the eastern extremity of the nave.

At Canterbury there were two apses, one at each end. The entrance to the church was through two doorways in the side walls opening into the lower portion of the nave. Each doorway was surmounted by a tower and contained an altar, that on the north side being dedicated to St. Martin, that on the south to St. Gregory. One of these chapels was used as a choir-room for the choristers, the other as a tribune. By the north doorway the monks

Entrance Gate, St. Augustine's, Canterbury.

entered from the cloisters; the faithful used the south doorway, as they came in from the churchyard or city. The archbishop had his throne at the end of the nave under the western apse, and his clergy sat round him at his feet. The Lady altar stood a few yards in front. From his great marble pulpit the prelate might be seen by the people, who stood behind between the first rows of pillars. Separated from them by a rail, the monks occupied the rest of the nave, while they sang office. Next was an open space containing a small altar—the *altare matutinale;* and behind it the entrance to the crypt, between two rows of steps leading to the *presbyterium.* Another small altar stood at the threshold of the sanctuary; and at the end of all, close up against the wall of the apse, rose the high altar built of rough masonry and dedicated to our Saviour. Tiny unglazed windows shed a feeble light on the walls, altars, tombs and shrines. Lamps in great number, and ever smoking censers, hung from large oak bosses in the roof. Round the eastern apse fell silken hangings, embroidered in gold and silver and mounted with precious stones and coloured beads; and paintings brought from the continent were nailed to the walls. The whole was a medley of eastern magnificence and barbaric ornament.*

Such was the Saxon cathedral that Eadmer knew in his boyhood; and it had changed but little since St. Augustine's day. Though in early times it was but of small size, it long remained the largest church in England; for, while the bishop was wont to carry out the Church's liturgy in his stone basilica, his monks in the country round had to be satisfied with rough structures of wood put together by Saxon carpenters. The walls of these were made of trunks of trees, sawed down the middle and

---

* Cf. Lingard, *History and Antiquities of the Anglo-Saxon Church*, p. 374; Morris, *Canterbury: Our Old Metropolis*, pp. 8, 9.

placed upright one against the other, with the bark still clinging to the outside ; a beam along the top and another along the bottom served as a framework to hold them together. Thatched straw or reeds formed the roof, and pieces of turf or wisps of hay filled up the chinks in the woodwork—such was the rude Saxon architecture of the day.

VII

CANTERBURY had now two monasteries, one outside the city governed by an abbot, and the other adjoining the cathedral under the immediate rule of the archbishop. Gradually the two houses became regularly constituted, and each had special features of its own.

St. Augustine's abbey, to give it the title which it bore in St. Dunstan's time and afterwards, was exempted from taxation by Ethelbert, and had also conferred upon it the *infangtheof*, or right of trying a thief taken in the act, the right of minting money, which it kept till king Stephen's reign, and later on the much valued privilege of holding a five days fair once a year. Its civil jurisdiction extended over six entire parishes, over portions of a hundred more, and even over certain quarters of the city. It had its own prison ; and by the irony of fate the prison remains to-day, though the abbey has long since fallen into ruins. In canonical status it was immediately under the Holy See, and was in no way subject to the archbishop's jurisdiction, who was the abbot's brother—not his superior. In his capacity of prelate the archbishop might not even enter the monastery save by consent of the community, and then only to offer mass or officiate at some liturgical function. After his election a newly appointed abbot would receive the primate's blessing ; but instead of

CANTERBURY CATHEDRAL IN SAXON TIMES

From *Canterbury: Our Old Metropolis*, by the late Father Morris. The plan is based on that contained in Willis's *Architectural History of Canterbury Cathedral*.

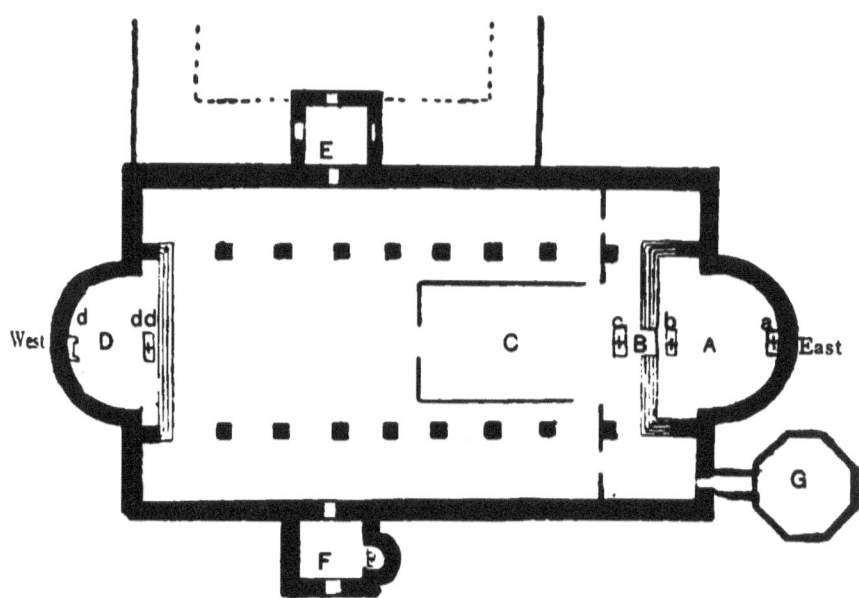

- A Presbyterium.
- B Entrance to the Crypt.
- C Choir.
- D Lady Chapel.
- E North Doorway. (St. Martin's.)
- F South Doorway. (St. Gregory's.)
- G St. John the Baptist.
- a High Altar.
- b Altar.
- c Altare Matutinale.
- d Archbishop's Throne.
- dd Altar.

The original Roman church we may assume to have been the parallelogram with the western apse and probably the two porches or small transepts. In this it would correspond in form with the little Roman church dedicated by St. Augustine to St. Pancras. The arrangement of the east end of the cathedral we may regard as Saxon, and in the main as St. Augustine's. The shape and precise position of St. John the Baptist's Chapel, built at the east end of the cathedral by Archbishop Cuthbert to serve as a baptistery and burial-place for the archbishops, are purely conjectural.

the abbot going to seek it, the archbishop would come in person and give it to him at the monastery. The abbot of St. Augustine's held precedence at general councils immediately after the abbot of Monte Cassino. He had a right to wear the mitre, sandals, gloves and other insignia of episcopal rank. Amongst the abbots in parliament he was only second to the abbot of St. Albans; for martyrs take precedence of confessors.

Christchurch enjoyed similar privileges. Having been the first monastery in England to which a bishop's see was attached, it long afforded a type, which was followed in the constitution of the chapters of many other dioceses. In these the monks formed the chapter, and the bishop was also the abbot, although in practice he was wont to delegate the authority belonging to that office to the prior. At the suppression of the monasteries under Henry VIII. the dioceses so constituted were Rochester, Durham, Norwich, Winchester, Bath, Ely, and Coventry. The arrangement caused a good deal of friction, especially in a metropolitan see; for from the very beginning of monastic life it had been the rule for the monks to nominate their own abbot, who in the case of Canterbury became archbishop also. Constant disputes occurred with suffragan bishops, who claimed a voice in the election; and the archbishop not infrequently quarrelled with his own monks owing to his confounding his jurisdiction as abbot with that of archbishop, or the goods of his see with those of the monastery. Hence an attempt was often made to establish a secular chapter in place of the monks. Nevertheless the basis on which Christchurch was constituted—it seems likely by St. Augustine himself—generally remained as a model which others sought to follow. In other sees the chapters of secular canons were frequently hotbeds of mischief and scandal. In such cases it was sometimes sought to replace them entirely by monastic chapters. Sometimes—but in England much less often—a middle course was taken, and canons regular were brought in; sometimes again the secular canons were bound to observe community life as a safeguard to their morals. In most cases, however, Canterbury was looked upon as an ideal which those engaged in reforming other Churches could not do better than follow.

The two abbeys stood side by side for nearly a thousand years—from A.D. 598 to 1538-9. This is not the place to tell their history with the sometimes amusing, often tragic, episodes of the differences in which rivalry between abbot and archbishop so often involved them. A single quarrel of exceptional bitterness might fill many pages in the old chronicles, while long years of peace and good will would make so little stir as scarcely to merit a single line.

Chapter V—ST. GREGORY'S LETTERS

I

ST. AUGUSTINE lost no time in telling the pope of the wonders accomplished in England. In the course of 598 [*] he despatched to Rome the priest Lawrence and the monk Peter. The pope immediately had the good news proclaimed throughout the length and breadth of the Church. He wrote it to Brunhild in France, and to the patriarch Eulogius in Egypt; [†] it was soon known as far as Constantinople. [‡] About that time he was retouching his homilies on Ezechiel, and he could not resist giving expression to his exuberant joy: "Lo, the tongue of Britain, which before could only utter barbarous sounds, has lately learned to make the *alleluia* of the Hebrews resound in praise of God. Lo, the ocean formerly so turbulent, lies calm and submissive at the feet of the saints; and its wild movements, which earthly princes could not control by the sword, are spellbound with the fear of God by a few simple words from the mouth of priests; and he who when an unbeliever never dreaded troops of fighting men, now that he believes fears the tongues of the meek. For by the words he has heard from heaven, and the miracles which shine around him, he receives the strength of the knowledge of God and is restrained by the fear of God, so that he is afraid to do wrong and yearns with his whole heart to come to the grace of eternity." [§]

---

[*] "Reversus in Britanniam. . . . misit *continuo*."—Bede, i. 27.
[†] Ep. xi. 62; viii. 30.   [‡] Ep. xi. 29.   [§] In Job, xxvii. 11.

Some time afterwards—we do not know the date—the pope despatched letters to England. One was for queen Bertha.* Gregory would not delay expressing his gratitude to her. He compared her to St. Helen, and exhorted her to complete her work with her royal spouse. Certain discreet reproofs show that in the mind of the pope the princess's zeal might have been more ardent, brought up in the faith as she had been. He concluded by saying that not in Rome alone were all eyes fixed upon her, but that her excellences had even reached the emperor's court at Constantinople.

Another letter was addressed to Augustine himself—a document unique in the history of ascetical literature. Gregory knew his friend and brother too well to marvel at at the miracles which accompanied his labours in England. Lawrence the priest had just informed him of them, and a shade of anxiety—of anxiety tempered with admiration—rose in his heart. He was about to crown the confidence he had already shown by giving the bishop the highest dignity on earth after the papacy itself; but first he sought to prevent any risk of pride. He had not a shadow of doubt about these miracles; for he refers to them time after time in his letters to others. Had he not believed in them, he would have had no reason to fear lest his dear wonder-worker should fall into the sin of vainglory ; yet it was fear of this that urged him to write the following letter :

" GREGORY TO AUGUSTINE, BISHOP OF THE ENGLISH.

"Glory to God in the highest, and on earth peace to men of good will ! For the grain of wheat which fell into the ground is dead and hath brought forth abundant fruit,† that so He should not reign alone in heaven, by whose death we live, by whose weakness we are strengthened, by

* Ep. xi. 29. † John xii. 24.

whose passion we are snatched from suffering, for whose love we seek in Britain brethren whom we knew not, of whose gift we have found those whom we sought without knowing them. But who here can tell what joy hath sprung up in the hearts of all the faithful since the English nation, through the working of the grace of Almighty God, and the labours of your Fraternity, hath been rid of the darkness of error, and overspread with the light of our holy Faith? For in perfect devotion this people now treads their idols under foot, whereunto in mad fear they have hitherto been subject; for they now worship God Almighty out of a pure heart; for recovered from the helplessness of their evil deeds, they are now bound by the strict rules of holy teaching; for now they are with all their mind subject to Divine precepts, and aided by the understanding of them; for now they are humbled even to the dust in prayer, that they may not grovel upon the earth. Whose work is this but His who saith, ' My Father worketh hitherto, and I work'?* Who, that He might shew Himself willing to convert the world, not in man's wisdom, but Himself by His own strength, chose men of no letters for the preachers whom he sent into the world. And this, too, He hath also done in this instance also, in that, among the English people, He hath deigned to perform deeds of strength through the infirmity of the weak.

"Howbeit, dear brother, there is in that heavenly gift what, in the midst of all our great joy, may well cause us to fear with an exceeding great fear. I well know that by the hands of your Affection, Almighty God hath wrought great miracles in the nation of which He would make choice. Need is there, then, that concerning this great heavenly gift you should at once rejoice while you fear, and fear while you rejoice. Rejoice assuredly you may, in that the souls of the English through outward miracles

* John v. 17.

are drawn towards inward grace; yet must you also fear lest, among the signs which are wrought by you, your feeble mind be lifted up into presumption of itself, and in proportion as it is exalted in honour from without, fall through vainglory from within. We ought to bear in mind that the disciples, when they returned with joy from preaching, and said unto the heavenly Master, 'Lord, even the devils are subject unto us in Thy name,' were straightway answered, 'In this rejoice not, but rather rejoice because your names are written in heaven.'* For they in rejoicing over miracles had set their hearts on a joy private and temporal. But from the private joy they are recalled to the public, from the temporal to the eternal, when it is said to them, 'In this rejoice, that your names are written in Heaven.' It is not all the elect who work miracles; howbeit all their names are kept written in heaven. For to the disciples of the Truth there should be no joy but on account of that good which they have in common with all, and wherein there is no end of their joy.

"It remains then, dearest brother, that, in the midst of those things which you do externally by the power of God, you should never cease from judging yourself discreetly within; and you should discreetly understand both concerning yourself, who you are, and likewise how high a grace is with this same nation, towards whose conversion you have been vouchsafed even the power of miracles. And if you remember yourself to have ever transgressed, whether in word or deed, in the sight of your Creator, call this continually to mind, to the end the remembrance of your guilt may repress the rising pride of your heart. And whatever power to do signs you shall receive, or have received, account not this as a gift to yourself, but rather to those for whose salvation such gifts have been vouchsafed you.

* Luke x. 20.

"And while on this subject it is impossible not to remember what happened in the case of one of God's servants, and one very precious in His sight. Moses, truly, while leading the people of God out of Egypt, wrought, as your Fraternity well knows, many wondrous signs in Egypt. And in his fast of forty days and nights on Mount Sinai, he received the Tables of the Law in the midst of lightnings and thunders, and while all the people feared greatly, he alone in service with Almighty God was joined with Him in familiar converse. Then opened he a path through the Red Sea, and had the pillar of a cloud as a guide in his way; when the people hungered, he brought them down manna from heaven, and by a miracle satisfied their desire, even to excess, with abundance of flesh in the wilderness. And then, when in the time of drought they came near a rock, his faith failed him, and he doubted whether he could bring water out of it; but at the word of the Lord he struck it, and the water burst forth in torrents. And, after this, how many miracles he wrought for thirty and eight years in the desert, who shall be able to account or find out? As often as any doubtful matter pressed on his mind, he entered into the tabernacle * and inquired of the Lord in secret, and was straightway instructed by the word of the Lord concerning the matter. And when the Lord was angry with the people, he appeased Him by the intervention of his prayers; and those who rose up in pride and made divisions among the people, he caused to to be swallowed up in the cavity of the yawning earth. The enemy he harassed by victories, and displayed signs among the people. But when at length he reached the Land of Promise, he was called up into the mount and was reminded of the sin he had committed thirty and eight years before, when he doubted of his power to bring forth the water. And he learned that for this he could not

* Exodus xxxiii. 9.

enter the Land of Promise. By this instance we learn how fearful a thing is the judgment of God Almighty, who wrought so many works by this His servant, yet kept his sin so long in remembrance.

"Therefore, dearest brother, if we must acknowledge that he who was thus especially chosen by Almighty God did still after so many signs die for his sin, what ought to be our fear, who know not as yet whether we be of the elect at all?

"Touching miracles which have been done by the reprobate, what shall I say to your Fraternity, who know so well the words which His Truth speaketh in the gospel? 'Many will say to Me in that day, Lord, have we not prophesied in Thy name, and cast out devils in Thy name, and done many miracles in Thy name? And then will I profess unto them, I never knew you: depart from Me, you that work iniquity.' Very great restraint, then, must be put on the mind in the midst of signs and miracles, lest, perchance, a man seek his own glory in these things, and rejoice with a merely private joy at the greatness of his exaltation. Signs are given for the gaining of souls, and towards His glory by whose power signs are wrought. One sign the Lord hath given us, wherein we may rejoice with exceeding joy, and whereby we may recognize in ourselves the glory of election,—' By this shall all men know that ye are My disciples, if ye have love one for another.'* And this sign the prophet sought when he said, 'Show me some token for good, that they who hate me may see and be ashamed.'†

"These things I say because I desire to bring down the mind of him who hears me to the depth of humility. But I know that your humility hath a just confidence of its own. I myself am a sinner; and I hold it in most

* John xiii. 35.   † Ps lxxxv. 17.

certain hope, that, by the grace of God, even our Lord Jesus Christ, our Almighty Creator and Redeemer, your sins have been already forgiven, and therefore you are in the number of the elect, so that the sins of others may be forgiven by you. Nor will your guilt bring sorrow in time to come, since your part it is to give joy in heaven by the conversion of many. He, the same our Creator and Redeemer, said, when speaking of the repentance of man, 'I say to you that even so there shall be joy in heaven upon one sinner that doth penance, more than upon ninty-nine just who need no penance.'* And if great joy, then, be in heaven over one penitent, what may we suppose that joy to be, when so vast a nation is converted from its error, and, coming to the faith, condemns by repentance all the evil that it hath done? Let us unite in this joy of the angels of heaven by concluding with these same words of angels with which we began. Let us say—let us one and all say, 'Glory to God in the highest, and on earth peace to men of good will.'" †

Is it conceivable that from this admirable letter Protestant writers should have drawn an argument in support of their favourite contention that Augustine was a proud man whose head was turned by success?

* Luke xv. 7.   † Lib. xi. Ep. 28.

II

IN 601 St. Augustine's two envoys, Peter and Lawrence, were again in Rome.* This time he sued for more labourers, for the harvest was growing greater, and the missionaries were all too few. They had too to lay before the pope certain cases of conscience or of administration which their bishop dared not resolve by himself, or for his solution of which he wished to have papal sanction.†

They found the pope suffering from an attack of gout, which made work difficult; so they merely reminded him of St. Augustine's mission and set to work to seek men who would join them. Twelve monks offered themselves, and many of these had in later years to play an important part in the history of England. Mellitus, who bore the title of abbot, afterwards founded the see of London, and Justus that of Rochester. Both in turn afterwards succeeded Lawrence on the throne of Canterbury. Paulinus had the glory of re-establishing the see of York, and carried the faith into Northumbria.

The pope loaded them with presents and alms. For Augustine and his priests there were sacred vessels, altar cloths, vestments—whatever was required for divine worship and the sacred ministry. There were relics; the chronicler Elmham speaks of fragments of the true cross, of the seamless coat, relics of the apostles, hairs of the Blessed Virgin, and—

---

* There must, it seems, have been two journeys—that of 598 (Bede, i. 27, says *misit continuo*), the object of which was to inform the pope of the success obtained, and that of 601. It is improbable that the envoys would have stayed in Rome in the interval, for they were so anxious to return at once that the pope had not time to write the letters he intended to Augustine. He excused himself on the score of his attack of gout—an excuse that could scarcely have served for three years.

† Ep. xi. 64. (In Hartmann's edition, xi. 56.)

who would believe it ?—a piece of Aaron's rod.* Moreover, there were books and manuscripts—the first library formed in Christian England. Many of these were works of great beauty : mediæval pilgrims who visited the abbey saw there the *Biblia Gregoriana*, written upon rose-coloured leaves showing strange reflections in the light. On a shelf above and behind the high altar, surrounded by reliquaries of every shape, were placed psalters, acts of the martyrs and books of the gospels, bound in chased silver and mounted with beryls and crystals—all presents from the great pope. It is possible that these books—these *primitiæ librorum*—even survived till the Reformation. The library of Corpus Christi at Cambridge and the Bodleian at Oxford possess two ancient books of the gospels said to have formed part of St. Gregory's gift.†

The monks were in a hurry to leave ; the pope, whose gout was no better, had not been able to settle the matters they had referred to his judgment. He waited to reply at leisure to Augustine's difficulties. On June 22, 601, he signed a large parcel of letters, which were delivered to the missionaries. ‡ There were some for all the bishops through whose sees they might have to travel—Marseilles,

---

* It should be noticed that we owe these details to the chronicler Elmham, who wrote as late as the fifteenth century. Bede only tells us in general terms that St. Gregory sent church plate and church furniture, vestments, relics and a number of books (*necnon et codices plurimos*). That in Elmham's time some objects were shown at St. Augustine's Abbey which could not have been sent by St. Gregory appears from the fact that Elmham's list of the presents includes "copes, one of which was blue." Now, as Mr. Bishop has recently shown in a very exhaustive article in the *Dublin Review*, the cope as a church vestment did not come into existence until many hundred years after the time of St. Gregory.

† Palæographical experts seem now to be agreed that neither of these MSS. can be as ancient as the time of St. Gregory.

‡ Ep. S. Greg. xi. 54-62.

Arles, Toulon, Gap, Vienne, Lyons, Châlons, Metz, Angers, Paris, and Rouen. Neither was Gregory unmindful of Brunhild and her grandchildren, or of Clotaire of Neustria. He urged the prelates and princes in their charity to give what assistance they could to the speedy accomplishment of the journey, for it is clear that delay weighed heavily on the envoys; and he begged that nothing might hinder them on the road.

III

LAWRENCE and Mellitus brought other letters for England. The most important of these was an open letter addressed to Augustine, which accompanied the gift of the pallium, appointed the saint primate of England, and regulated the division of that country into ecclesiastical provinces.

The pallium is a long band of white wool, worn over the pontifical vestments. It is the symbol of union with Rome as rightful mistress of all the Churches. Before being sent to the prelate who is destined to receive it, it is left for a night on St. Peter's tomb. Then, as though impregnated with the spirit of the apostle, it becomes much more than a mere ornament: it forms part, as it were, of the very mantle of the bishop of bishops, and is the mark of a most exalted jurisdiction; a sort of participation in our Lord's commission to St. Peter—*Feed My sheep.*

So Augustine became metropolitan; his Church possessed the visible sign of union with Rome, whence all jurisdiction flows. Later on the pallium became a charge on the arms of the archiepiscopal see of Canterbury. To this day the pall argent on an azure field may be seen on the keystone of every arch in the old cathedral, in its windows and on the archbishops' tombs. Just as the words *fidei defensor* on Her Majesty's coins recall with grim irony the faith of other days, so on every deed he signs must the Anglican archbishop set the mark of Rome.

Over whom, and how, in the intention of the pope, was Augustine to exercise this high jurisdiction? The letter is precise in its instructions, but in the issue they were not carried out. We must remember that as yet there existed at Rome only a most imperfect idea of England. Too much reliance was placed on a confused recollection of the organization of the British Church in the time of the Romans, when York and London each had its bishop. It was believed that the island enjoyed a certain political unity which was far from really existing.

"We grant you leave," said St. Gregory, "to ordain twelve bishops in different places, who shall be subject to your jurisdiction, so far that the bishop of London shall always in future be consecrated by his own synod and receive the honour of the pallium from this holy and apostolic see which by God's appointment I serve. To the city of York we desire that you send a bishop, whomsoever you determine to ordain, provided that if the same city with the neighbouring places receive the word of God, he also may ordain twelve bishops and enjoy the dignity of metropolitan; for to him also, if our life be spared, we propose by favour of the Lord to give the pallium; yet we wish him to be subject to the direction of your Fraternity. After your death let him preside over the bishops whom he has ordained without being in any way subject to the jurisdiction of the bishop of London. Let the bishops of London and York in future divide the honour, so that the first ordained may have precedence; but let them arrange together by common counsel and harmonious action whatever is to be done out of zeal for Christ."

So the purpose of Gregory was to establish two equal provinces, London and York, each comprising twelve sees. On this first point it is a remarkable fact that the papal will was not carried out till just before the schism, when by the erection of some new sees there were twenty-four bishops, although unevenly distributed between York and Canterbury. Moreover St. Gregory wished one of the two archbishoprics to be fixed at London; this was doubtless to restore the broken chain of the former hierarchy. Perhaps in Italy they still believed in the prosperity of the old commercial capital. Alas! London was then a heap of ruins, amid which a little Saxon colony was beginning to settle.

The pope ruled moreover that in the future the senior archbishop should have precedence of the other. Meanwhile the entire primacy was for St. Augustine—a sort of personal primacy. The division of authority between the two metropolitans was to date only from his death. However, Augustine was not bishop of London; the pope did not assign to him any particular see, but doubtless left him free to place it where he pleased.

The sequel greatly modified the pope's arrangements. In the first place London was never made an archbishopric. St. Augustine nominated a bishop to it, but three sees, London, Rochester, and Canterbury, were too few to make a province. Augustine died, and matters remained as they were, the metropolitan keeping provisionally his see at Canterbury. The conversion of England did not make the progress that was hoped. It was only by slow degrees that an approach was made to the number of bishoprics fixed by St. Gregory; a hundred years later there were still but fifteen. So the provisional arrangement became final. Not till centuries afterwards did the bishop of London receive the third rank in the hierarchy—not indeed till the city had regained under the Normans its former importance; under the Saxons London remained one of the most obscure of the English sees. The old trading capital seems to have been quite resigned to its humble rank. It was not so with York; for many ages a disorderly and often scandalous struggle was maintained between the two metropolitans.

The letter of St. Gregory to St. Augustine ended thus: " You, brother, are to have subject to you by the authority of our Lord Jesus Christ not only those bishops whom you have ordained, nor those only who have been ordained by the bishop of York, but likewise all the priests of Britain, that they may take from your Holiness's lips and life their pattern of right belief and pious living, and performing their duty in faith and morals may attain to the heavenly kingdom when God wills. God keep you safe, most reverend brother."

Thus Augustine's primacy was made as wide-reaching as possible. Out of the fulness of his authority over the universal Church the pope made him head not only of the newly-founded Churches, but also of those British Churches of which for many years past so little had been heard at Rome.

IV

AS might have been expected, the pope also addressed a letter to king Ethelbert. It was written in that weighty and authoritative style which he knew so well how to combine with bright touches of his own.

" TO THE MOST NOBLE LORD, OUR VERY EXCELLENT SON, ETHELBERT, KING OF THE ENGLISH, GREGORY, BISHOP.

" Almighty God places good men to govern peoples that by their means He may dispense the gifts of His lovingkindness to all those over whom they are set to rule. We are aware that this is so in the English nation, over which your Highness has been placed for this very purpose that through the blessings granted to yourself the blessings of heaven may be bestowed on the nations subject to you. And therefore, most noble son, with earnest care keep in the grace you have received from God; hasten to spread the Christian faith amongst the peoples under your rule; redouble your righteous zeal in their conversion, drive out the worship of idols, overthrow the walls of their temples, build up your subjects' morals with great cleanness of life, by exhorting, terrifying, praising, correcting, and by setting an example of good deeds; so that in heaven you may have Him for your rewarder, whose name and knowledge you will have spread upon earth. For He whose honour you seek and maintain among the heathen will make the glory of your name yet more glorious with posterity."

Just as the pope had compared queen Bertha to St. Helen, so now he proposes to Ethelbert the example of Constantine. The parallel was doubtless very imperfect; but the first Christian emperor had been so courageous as to break with the traditions of persecution in the past, and had influence enough to draw whole peoples in his wake. The Church left the rest to God, and the pope chose to consider only the great benefits he had brought upon the world.

Next he proceeded to praise Augustine: "Our most reverend brother bishop Augustine has been trained under monastic rule, is filled with knowledge of holy scripture, and by God's grace is endowed with good works; to whatever he advises you, listen, act upon it with devotion, and keep it in mind. For if you listen to him in what he speaks on behalf of the Lord Almighty, the same God

Almighty will the more readily listen to him when he prays on your behalf. For if, which God forbid, you neglect his words, how will Almighty God be able to hear him on your behalf whom you neglect to hear in God's behalf? Hold fast to him therefore with all your mind in the fervour of faith, and aid his efforts by the power which God gives you, so that He may make you a sharer in His kingdom, since you cause His faith to be received and cherished in your own."

Then the pope insists upon the thought, which haunts him, of the approaching end of the world. "For," said he, "many things hang over us which were never before. If any of these things take place in your country, be not troubled in mind, for these signs of the end of the world are sent beforehand to us that we may be solicitous about our souls, may be watchful for the hour of death, and when the Judge shall come, may be found prepared by good deeds."

The letter to Ethelbert ended with words touching for their fatherly simplicity: "I send you some small presents, which will not be small to you, since you will receive them from the blessing of the holy apostle Peter."

These gifts consisted of a golden vessel, a silver dish, an embroidered shirt, a military cloak of silk, a golden mirror, a saddle, and a bridle set with gold and pearls. Ethelbert afterwards bequeathed these tokens of the great pope's friendship to the treasury of St. Peter's abbey; in the middle ages they were still shown among the relics of the monastery.

In his letter to Ethelbert there was a passage which on reflection the pope found to be too strong—that in which he spoke of destroying the temples. In the day of the Church's triumph her practice in this matter had not been uniform. Constantine, while he promised toleration, destroyed the pagan shrines, since policy or morals required it. Sometimes, as at Alexandria, the crowd took the matter into their own hands, or perhaps a saint, as Martin of Tours, led in person the attack upon idols. In other places it was thought sufficient to exorcize the temples. A council held at Carthage decreed that any temple which added to the beauty of a town should be left standing. A law of Honorius enacted that they should be converted into churches, and this is what St. Benedict did with the temple of Apollo at Monte Cassino. Rome herself set an example of toleration: the temple of Janus was still frequented in the sixth century; the Pantheon was only exorcized in 610.

St. Gregory thought that it might be possible to make use of some of the pagan temples without destroying them. That surely was the most reasonable course; for the common-people is naturally averse to change, and clings to places and customs with a veneration which is seldom so strong amongst the educated and cultured. By destroying the old temples the king would in many cases have trampled upon heathen prejudice without any good result. It was much better to convert what might not be destroyed and to tolerate what was not in itself wrong.

The new band of missionaries had quitted Rome and must already have reached France. So the pope sent a messenger to Mellitus with the following letter:

"Tell Augustine what I have long been turning over in my mind concerning the English, that the idol temples in that nation should by no means be destroyed. But the idols themselves that are in them should be destroyed; let water be blessed and sprinkled in these same temples, altars built and relics set there. For if the temples are well built, they should be converted from the worship of devils to the service of the true God, so that the people when they see that their temples are not destroyed, may put error from their hearts, and knowing and adoring the true God, may assemble with less sense of novelty in their wonted places."

It will be remembered that Augustine had already acted on the principle laid down by St. Gregory, when he dedicated to St. Pancras the little sanctuary where Ethelbert had formerly offered sacrifice. The pope now went on to give a wider application to his decision. He had heard tell of certain Saxon customs, such as their great festivals at the two solstices and at harvest time; the sacrifices which took place in September, when the sacred precincts were thronged with folk who ate and drank, shouted and danced in honour of their gods before the altars, loaded with victims; of the night-watching of the women; of the January masques, when they dressed in skins of deer or bullocks, and covered their heads with heads of beasts. So Gregory continued:

"And since that people is wont to offer large numbers of oxen in sacrifice to devils, some change of festival should be devised for them in this matter also; say, that on the dedication-day of those churches which were formerly used as heathen temples, or on the feast of the holy martyrs whose relics are placed there, they should set up round those churches booths made with branches of trees, and keep the festivals with religious rejoicing. And let them no longer sacrifice animals to the devil; but they may slaughter them to God's honour for their own food, and return thanks out of their fulness to the Giver of all things, so that by keeping some outward rejoicings they may more easily be led to the joys of the soul. For it is without doubt impossible to wean hard hearts from everything at once, and he who tries to go up a height rises by paces and steps, and not by bounds. Thus the Lord made Himself known to the people of Israel in Egypt; but He retained for His own worship the use of sacrifices, which they were wont to offer to the devil,* and commanded them to offer animals in sacrifice to Him. . . . In your charity you must tell this to our aforesaid brother, so that, having regard to his present position, he may consider how to arrange all these matters. May God hold you safe in His keeping, most beloved son."

These instructions, so full of tender consideration, were quite in the spirit of the saint. Elsewhere on a dedication festival he bade his subdeacon prepare a great feast for the poor, and buy at the price of ten gold pieces thirty flagons of wine, two hundred lambs, two barrels of oil, twelve sheep and a hundred chickens.†

St. Gregory's counsels were followed, at least in part. The old Roman churches and former temples were devoted to Christian worship. It is alleged that on the site of St. Paul's in London there formerly stood a temple to Diana, and on that of Westminster abbey another to Apollo. A number of churches, especially in Kent, have Roman foundations. Later on the compilers of the Durham Ritual and Egbert's Pontifical sought to carry out Gregory's intentions by including forms for the consecration to Christian worship of pagan vessels found amongst old ruins. Christian festivals took the place of some of those kept by the heathen, and sometimes even received their Saxon name. It was so with the days of the week. Easter again was the feast of the goddess Eastre, kept in April; and Christmas was formerly Yule, the name of the festival kept by the Saxons at the winter solstice.

It was perhaps a little imprudent to counsel that religious feasts should be brought to a close with profane banquetings. For a long time attempts of this kind had failed; St. Ambrose at Milan, St. Augustine at Hippo, and the popes at Rome had been obliged to interfere and

* Levit. xvii. 7.   † Ep. i. 56.

forbid practices which changed the churchyards and even
the churches themselves into places of noisy and sometimes
sinful revelry. St. Gregory rather strained a point in
his desire to make the road to the faith both wide and
easy. In this and several other matters experience has
shown that it would have been better to keep to common
rules; for the Saxons were not more barbaric than the
Germans of the continent. In 747 the council of Clovesho
had to decide in favour of greater strictness of practice;
it complained that at the Rogations games, horse-racing
and feasting were mixed up with the religious
ceremonies. It was the more necessary to put a stop to
such abuses since the English clergy of that day were
much inclined to their national vice of drunkenness.
" That," said Boniface, " is the curse of our race."

V

S T. GREGORY'S letter to Mellitus concluded with
the answer which the pope was at last able to give
to St. Augustine's questions. These he sent by the same
messenger. In spite of the evident haste with which this
famous document was put together, we may trace there many
of the most striking features of Gregory's character. In it we
may see reflected the pontiff whose views were as broad as
they were sublime; the former magistrate whose decisions
were framed with all the precision of the law; the true
father of the English Church, condescending to the needs
of his newborn child.*

* The authenticity of these answers has been much disputed. Even
St. Boniface, when he happened to meet a certain Saxon who quoted
Gregory's decision in defence of a certain matrimonial dispensation,
expressed a doubt of their genuineness. He wrote to Rome asking
that a careful search should be made for the document in the
archives; when it was not forthcoming, he enquired at Canterbury
through the learned archbishop Nothelm whether it had really come

The questions put show us both the special difficulties of foreign missions in the seventh century, and the reflections which the monks might have made in travelling for the first time beyond the Roman campagna; their surprise, perhaps their scandal and hesitation, when they had to choose between Roman usages and those they may have noted on their way. Sometimes it is Augustine himself who hesitates; sometimes he only asks for a papal decision to confirm his own views, as is remarked by Gregory himself. It was natural for the head of the mission to have doubts and to refer to his superior for their solution. At this, however, some Anglican historians have seen fit to take offence. In their foolish desire to belittle the founder of the English Church, they see in this course a sign of weakness. Being unable to show that he was not the

from St. Gregory. Nothelm replied that the practice of the English Church in the matter of the dispensation was the very contrary. Venerable Bede at the same date had not the same scruples, and did not hesitate to insert in his history the text we now possess. He also was acquainted with the English practice; but, being doubtless better informed than Nothelm himself, he knew that many things prescribed by St. Gregory had not the force of law, since circumstances prevented their being applied. The fact that the document was not found among the pontifical archives in St. Boniface's day has driven many critics of repute to deny its authenticity. "The letter is certainly spurious," says Duchesne *(Origines du Culte Chrétien,* p. 94). But Ludwig Hartmann, the latest editor of St. Gregory's Letters, holds that it is genuine *(Monumenta Germ. Hist.* Epist. S. Greg. ii. p. 331). Mommsen thinks that we only have extracts. Others regard the document as a redaction of notes from the pope's verbal instructions taken down by Lawrence on the spot (Grisar, S.J., *Civiltà Cattolica,* 1892, ii. p. 46). Jaffé *(Regesta,* 1885, p. 699) classes it among the authentic letters. Père Brou is inclined to accept the tradition. It may be added that Dom F. A. Gasquet and Mr. Edmund Bishop in an essay privately printed in Rome have defended the genuineness of the letters (cf. *Tablet,* May 8, 1897); and the Anglican Canon Mason in his *Mission of St. Augustine* favours the same conclusion.

docile instrument of Rome, they seek to detract from his merit and his virtues as much as possible. That genius was on the side of St. Gregory is evident; that Augustine committed faults is possible. But he is reproached with having presumed to work miracles, with having maintained his dependence on Rome, with having introduced the Latin liturgy, with narrowness of mind as well as with rashness and presumption, with arrogance and intolerance as well as with timidity and vacillation. The pope had a different opinion of the man whom he dragged from the peaceful retreat of a monastery to entrust with the carrying out of his fondest dream. To detract from St. Augustine is to detract from St. Gregory. Nevertheless the secret of this baseless antipathy on the part of some English Protestants to the apostle of their island is very simple: to them Augustine spells Rome, and Rome is an enemy of whose pretensions and encroachments they live in constant dread.

The first difficulty that required solution was the organization of the bishop's household. In the journey through Gaul the missionaries had noticed that the priests did not live apart from the bishops as they did in Italy; yet did they not live according to the strict monastic life instituted at Vercelli by St. Eusebius, nor even as in Africa, where priests lived in community, and were bound in practice by religious vows, although they were not monks. In Gaul an intermediate practice prevailed: the clergy lived a common but not a religious life; all the canons took their meals at the bishop's table. In consequence they no longer had a right, as in Italy, to a quarter of the offertories for their maintenance. What rule was it best to adopt at Canterbury?

Then there was diversity of rite, especially in the celebration of mass. Instead of the Roman ceremonies of which our present mass is only a sort of condensation, the missionary monks had been present in Gaul at long litanies and a great number of lessons which were strange to them. They had also seen processions in which the elements before consecration were carried about among the faithful almost with the same marks of respect as the Eucharist itself—the bread in a vessel shaped like a tower, the wine in a chalice. The Host was broken into nine portions, each of which was meant to represent a mystery in our Saviour's life. Accustomed as they were to regard the prayers and acts prescribed by the liturgy as symbols of the faith, they failed to see how unity of faith was consistent with a diversity of use, or why so great a difference should exist between Rome and Gaul in the celebration of the very mass. It was a prudent question and of more practical importance than appears at first sight; for the English of Canterbury, who had so lately assisted in St. Martin's church at the Gallican rites observed by queen Bertha's chaplain, may perhaps have wondered how the Roman monks, though they had different uses, could yet preach the same faith.

In Augustine's questions may be seen the special difficulties to be met with in a Church which is not yet organized. Augustine was bishop, but what was to be his position in regard to the hierarchies of Gaul and Britain?* He was living in a remote part of the world, quite cut off from his nearest neighbours; he had to lay the foundation of a hierarchy and therefore would have to consecrate his colleagues; but he was alone and had nowhere to look for assistant prelates. Then there were penalties for certain crimes to be considered: Roman law punished theft with double or quadruple restitution; in other countries the Salic law required as much as tenfold:

* This and the following question, so natural if put by St. Augustine, would be difficult to account for if they belonged to a later age.

what was he to do with cases of sacrilegious theft? Then there were impediments to marriage, which always vary in different countries; the Anglo-Saxons even allowed union between brothers and sisters-in-law, and between stepmothers and stepsons. The custom prevailed, especially in royal families, of a son marrying his father's widow, if she were not also his own mother.

The pope took each question in turn. He wished the clergy at Canterbury to follow as nearly as possible the custom of the primitive Church. The bishop therefore should live in common with his monks without any division of offerings. That was the rule that Gregory had established at his own house, which was more like a monastery than a pontifical palace.

In the matter of the liturgy he wished Augustine not to be exclusive. "You know, brother, the custom of the Roman Church, in which you remember that you were reared. But I should like you carefully to pick out anything that you have found which may be more pleasing to Almighty God, whether in the Roman, or Gallican, or any other Church; and to introduce by the best arrangement into the Church of the English, which is still new to the faith, what you have been able to gather from many Churches. For things are not to be loved on account of places, but places are to be loved on account of good things. From every Church then choose those things which are pious, religious, and right, and having collected them as it were in a bundle, lay them in the minds of the English to form a custom."

Some authors have considered this strange concession, as they deem it, sufficient to prove that the letter is spurious. "No Roman, certainly no pope, could have written the passage, *Things are not to be loved on account of places*, etc.*" The papacy at this period, they hold, far

---

* Cf. Duchesne, *Origines du Culte Chrétien*, p. 94.

from favouring the formation of new liturgies, was seeking to restore unity with the ritual of Rome for a basis—a unity which was compromised by the adoption of oriental customs in many Churches of the west. But St. Gregory was not one of those timid souls who are driven along by the breezes of opinion. He possessed keen powers of perception, and he had travelled; we need not wonder then that he marched so far ahead of his age as sometimes to alarm the short-sighted. If he authorized his disciple to choose from one source or another usages out of which to form, not a new liturgy, but a *proprium*, while other Churches must follow the Roman rite, he had himself set the example. To certain persons who found fault with changes he had made in received uses, and imagined that they smacked too much of the east, he replied: "The Church of Constantinople and any other may have good rites and ceremonies. For myself, just as I correct my subordinates when convicted of any fault, so am I ready to follow them if they do well. He is a fool who lets his primacy prevent him wishing for information respecting what is better." He had followed the lead of a Gaulish Church in organizing at Rome the processions known for distinction's sake as the *Litaniæ Majores*, and he told St. Leander concerning different rites of baptism that, "as to triple immersion, so long as there is unity of faith mere differences of custom count for nothing." *

What other answer might Gregory have given? When the missionaries should come in contact with the British Churches, what were they to do? Should they seek to impose on them the Roman use in all respects, or were they to abandon this in favour of the British? It was proved in the end that the spirit of condescension was the spirit of wisdom. Had all those concerned been less unbending, there might have been spared many a bitter

* Ep. ix. 12; i. 45.

struggle which gave scandal to men rather than glory to God.

It was decided that the missionaries should keep their Roman liturgy; but they borrowed details both from the Gallicans and from the Irish. These, however, presently disappeared in the great movement for unification which took place under the first Carolingians.

St. Gregory next gives Augustine permission to consecrate the first bishops of the new Church without the presence of two assistant bishops, as required by canon law; but he must found his new sees near enough to one another to make it unnecessary again to have recourse to this exceptional practice. The new hierarchy was to be independent of the Frankish bishops. Augustine, primate of England, was not to exercise jurisdiction across the Channel; but he might take council with the archbishop of Arles to remedy any abuses he should observe in the Gallican Church. He was not to put his sickle into his neighbour's corn, but he might as he passed rub some ears with his hand and eat, that is to say, might exhort with all discretion and charity. The pope wrote also to the archbishop of Arles that if Augustine should travel in Gaul he should take account of any observations that the English bishop might make to him. "For it often happens," said he, "that strangers in spite of distance quickly learn of disorders committed afar off."

In case of sacrilegious theft the restitution was to be pure and simple; the Church should not make profit out of her temporal losses, nor enrich herself out of men's folly. A magnanimous and noble decision, but too gentle for the rude barbarians whom the Church had to conquer. We shall see later how king Ethelbert punished the same crime. The pope, however, is not satisfied with giving a bare reply to the question; he raises the matter to a higher level, and tells Augustine in what spirit he should punish. He was to act in the spirit of charity, like a father who chastises his child but nevertheless makes him his heir.

As regards marriages the pope decided that two brothers might marry two sisters, but that a man might not marry his sister-in-law nor a stepson his stepmother. However, as the missionaries have to deal with barbarians who may have contracted these marriages before baptism without knowing their wickedness, the Church uses gentleness. Sometimes indeed she chastises strongly, but that is in the case of those who may dare to relapse into pagan ways; these shall be excommunicated. Sometimes she tolerates and feigns not to see, but this is done to attain more surely the suppression of the evil. Thus acted St. Paul, who said to his new-born faithful, " I have fed you with milk, not with strong meat." So the neophytes who may have been formerly married in this way shall be admonished to abstain, but shall not be debarred from the holy table. However, such marriages are to be absolutely forbidden to the faithful.

Part of Gregory's concessions remained a dead letter. From their own experience the archbishops of Canterbury thought fit to contract the limits and conform to the customs of the universal Church, which was disposed to add to the impediments already laid down by Roman law. St. Boniface was astonished in the eighth century at meeting with a man who alleged that he had leave to marry his uncle's widow in spite of the immemorial law of the English Church. The Gregorian dispensations seem by that date to have been forgotten.

The pope turned next to certain relics of Judaism which still tainted the canon law and penitential books of that day. He did not suppose, he replied, that on this point Augustine could have had the least hesitation; he doubtless only wished to shelter himself behind pontifical

* Ep. ix. 68.

authority. Why refuse baptism to a woman with child and make a crime of her fruitfulness? Why keep from church a woman after childbirth, and punish her for her pains? If an idolater, why not baptize at once both the woman and her offspring, both of whom childbirth places in danger of death? Why apply to the woman certain obsolete Mosaic regulations, and add to the humiliations of nature those of the ancient law?

By this letter Gregory and his envoy teach barbarous nations the respect due to woman. Descending to details which "our modern prudishness would not tolerate," he sketches rules for preachers to follow. "For," remarked Augustine, "with the English it is necessary to speak out on every point in a way that they shall understand." The pope explains to husbands the duties they owe to those who have just become mothers; he reminds mothers that they should suckle their children and not hand them over to strange nurses from laziness or from motives still less justifiable. He lays down for his dear English the fundamental laws of Christian marriage. He tries "to impress deep in the heart of the Saxon wife every duty of woman, at the same time that he marks her place in the Christian family, lifts her to higher dignity, and safeguards her modesty."* He goes further, and lays the foundation of saintliness; he desires that those barbarians, whom he treats as children, be taught the tender virtue of chastity. The missionaries need no longer trouble to apply to the letter the precepts of the old law in the matter of legal defilements; let them seek only its spirit. If it happen that a person be inspired by a fervent love for the Eucharist, he is not therefore to be blamed; and if he abstain through a reasonable scruple, the respect he shows is praiseworthy. "For," he says, "it is usual for noble souls to see a fault where there is no

* Montalembert.

fault; what is done through no fault often has its source in a fault; so, if we are hungry it is no sin to eat, but it was the sin of Adam that caused our hunger."

The pope's letter was wide in its range, embracing as it did diocesan administration, bishop's jurisdiction, liturgy, marriage and the religious life. It was Rome's charter to the faithful in England, raising them to the dignity of a Church and laying down the principles of the new Church's constitution and organization. It was only left for Augustine to extend the field of his apostolate and to seek on all sides for fellow-workers.

Chapter VI—THE WELSH CHURCH

I

THE time now seemed to have come for joining hands with the Churches in the west of the island. Ethelbert's kingdom had so grown by annexation that it already stretched from the North Sea to the Severn. Without ever quitting the king's dominion it was possible to travel to the border of Wales. Augustine availed himself of the facility which this gave to his mission.

It was now the year 602 or 603. The magnificent Roman roads led our saint by London to a point beyond Bath. There on the great estuary of the Severn, at the mouth of the Avon, is a little village which still bears the saint's name—Aust, *trajectus Augustini*,—a small parish embracing the spot which from time immemorial has been the starting-point of the ferry plying between Gloucestershire and South Wales.

Augustine was here on Saxon ground. The plain of Gloucester towards the north had been in Saxon hands since 584; but the Welsh territories were not far distant. Two days journey to the south might have brought him to the famous shrine of Glastonbury, founded—so ran the legend—by Joseph of Arimathea, built of wickerwork by angels, consecrated by Jesus Christ Himself. The Welsh primate, St. David of Menevia, had lately made it into a monastery.

There is no reason to believe that Augustine passed by Glastonbury, but at Bath he might have observed the ruins of one of the twelve monasteries founded by the same holy

bishop. This had been destroyed almost immediately
after it was built. Opposite to where Augustine stood,
on the further bank of the Severn, rose the Welsh hills and
the outskirts of the great forest of Dean. At the top
of every hill and in the recesses of every valley were hidden
hermitages, convents and churches; a few miles from the
ferry was the monastery of Caer Gwent, the Venta Silurum
of the Romans; behind it was Llancarvan, once the home
of St. Cadoc; then Caerleon, an ancient episcopal see,
which had been abandoned a little time before. In olden
days Caerleon had sent its bishop to the council of Arles.
Then came Llandaff, whose old church still lays claim to
St. Lucius, that half-legendary British king.

Augustine perhaps thought that under authority from
Rome things would right themselves and that his proposals,
which were fair and reasonable, would be accepted without
question. It was necessary to combine in the work of evangelizing the island; but certain differences in liturgy and discipline stood in the way of united action, and these must be
removed. The saint, however, was mistaken, and the hour
was ill-chosen.

II

THE WELSH Church was passing though a crisis. It
is not now easy to describe its condition in detail on
account of difficulties in chronology; for a student seeking
to assign dates to bishops whose legends alone have come
down to us, is confronted with divergences of twenty or
thirty years or more. He alights on bishops' sees which
after being founded and transferred are lost to sight;
on lists of bishops which give a name or two and then
break off abruptly, to resume with names dating two or
three centuries later.

In the middle of the sixth century when the great shock

of invasion had ceased, there existed an organized Church, having numerous and constantly changing dioceses, mostly grouped round the monasteries whose abbots were also their bishops. Bishops were frequently consecrated without any fixed sees; these travelled from place to place and founded dioceses as circumstances permitted. Later on, about the year 580, a fearful epidemic seems to have attacked Wales, which lasted several years and carried off a tenth of the population. A great number emigrated in the wake of their clergy and bishops and took refuge on the continent. In 596 St. Teilo, bishop of Llandaff, gathered together what remained of his emigrant flock and ventured to return to his diocese. Everywhere he found the Church scattered and in ruins. It was necessary to rebuild from foundation to roof; so he consecrated bishops and sent them forth over the country to organize dioceses according to the needs of clergy and faithful.*

How had this work of restoration progressed when seven or eight years later Augustine presented himself at Llandaff? How many dioceses had been restored? Where was St. Teilo? How many bishops were there in the country? It is impossible to answer these questions with any certainty.

Again, what was the character of the Welsh clergy? The lamentations of Gildas have come down to us: "Britain has priests, but they are mad; she has plenty of them, but they are unchaste; she has a clergy, but they are cunning thieves; she has bishops, it is said, but they are mere wolves ready to slay their sheep, heedless of their people's good, only concerned with filling their own bellies. They have churches, but they only go there to win a base pay. They instruct the people, but offer them the example of their own vices and misbehaviour. They seldom

---

* Liber Llandavensis.

approach the altar, and never with a clean heart. They never chide the people for their sins, for they commit as many themselves. They hate truth as an enemy, and love falsehood with a brother's love. They look down upon the good who are poor as vermin; but wealthy scoundrels they honour like angels. . . . They hunger more to rise a step in the hierarchy than to gain the kingdom of heaven. They stand with gaping mouths like idiots when they are taught the science of the saints; but their ears itch for the follies and fables of the world."

Gildas is writing about the secular clergy. The picture he paints is doubtless more gloomy than truth required, and he has plainly yielded to the temptation of gaining effect by using sharp contrasts. But though we make every allowance, the result is sad enough. Had the clergy reformed during the last years of the century? Was Augustine confronted by a simoniacal priesthood, addicted to luxury and vice?

But let us not forget the monks. It might have been questioned whether these did not belong to another race and to another Church. The Welsh Thebaid glowed with intense supernatural life. Vast numbers joined the religious state; Llan Elwy had a community of nine hundred and fifty; Llandaff of a thousand; Bangor y Coed of two thousand one hundred. A village of wooden huts or of cells dug out of the soft rock, the whole enclosed within a ditch and palisade, formed the monastery. In the offices of the Church choir succeeded to choir, and Latin psalms were sung unceasingly night and day.

In accordance with St. David's rule all rose at cockcrow. They prayed till it was time to begin to work; then, clad in skins, they went forth into the fields, where they spent the day. They lived by their labour; the monastery received absolutely nothing from those who left the world to join it. The monks kept unbroken silence, and, so far as human weakness allowed them, prayed unceasingly. They used no oxen to lighten their labour. When evening came, a frugal supper was prepared for them; for they had not yet broken their fast. The meal consisted of bread, roots, salt, water, and milk. Three hours prayer brought the day to a close. Before a postulant was deemed fit to enter upon so mortified a life, he was required to beg for ten days at the monastery-gateway the favour of admission; and his requests were met with refusal—almost with rudeness.

Then when grace urged a monk to increase his austerities, he would go forth to seek a convent where the rule was more strict. Others buried themselves in the mountains, or took refuge on rocky islets in the sea. There in solitude they spent day and night singing psalms or making repeated genuflections, sometimes plunged to the waist in icy cold water.

In happened in time that the tide of sanctity overflowed from Wales into Ireland, where St. Patrick's work was beginning to decline. David of Menevia planted there a new garden of virtues. He became the father of that second generation of saints which, tradition tells us, shone as the moon, coming midway between the age of St. Patrick, which blazed as the sun, and that of St. Colman, which was beautiful as the stars.

We should like to know more of the life led by those great communities of monks. Perhaps we should find therein an explanation of the strange obstinacy which for two centuries gave monastic life in Wales so sad a fame and plunged her Church into schism the most absurd. When St. German of Auxerre came to reform the British Church, he saw that the root of mischief lay in the lack of instruction, and founded schools. Ignorance, combined with a foolish conservatism, produced a harvest of evils. Let us not forget too that fortune had pent up the Welsh within a distant corner of the world; that for more than a century the heathen nations on their flank had cut them off from the main army of Christendom. Communication with other Churches and that free flow of thought which serves to impart breadth of mind and to cut off the narrow prejudices of race or nation, had long been impossible for them. Then the Britons had long been weaned from Greco-Roman civilization; it would be impossible to reckon how much the Italian, Gallic, and Spanish races had gained from their long-standing devotion to letters and classical art; for clearness of perception, a delicate sense of the differences in things, and wealth of ideas all result from contact of mind with mind. The Celtic races of the north gave no doctors to the Church, and what remains of their literature leaves but a poor impression of intellectual worth. Take Gildas as an example. He is eloquent, but he is chiefly imaginative. A race of bards and solitaries, the Celts lacked a strong theological foundation.

Moreover in character they were still akin to barbarism. Side by side with men of high saintliness were others gross and brutal, and such also sought refuge in the convents. The penitential canons take for granted that there might be found therein monks who were thieves and gluttons; one man refuses to work, another comes to office with his tongue swollen from drunkenness. To train them to religious life and to teach them habits of meekness and chastity, there was no end to the mortifications, fasts and long periods of seclusion to which they had to submit. As a result the monasteries peopled the land with pious hermits and solitaries of marvellous sanctity; but the learning they imparted was of the most trivial and imperfect kind.

Both the secular clergy, whose lives were so little in keeping with their calling, and the monks, whose fervour was too often accompanied by ignorance and obtuseness, still clung to many ancient uses. For long they had advanced step by step with the rest of the western Church: they had accepted the canons which were sent them by Rome; they had changed the date for the observance of Easter with pope Leo; and afterwards, in company with Gaul, Spain, and northern Italy, abandoned the papal liturgy in favour of the eastern rite which reached them from Milan.* Then the Saxon invasion put an end to their relations with the rest of Christendom. On the continent the Church continued to develope both in liturgy and discipline. When outward communion was restored, the Celtic Church was more than a hundred years behind her sisters. She had her own uses and traditions, venerable for their antiquity, and therefore of a kind with which it is always imprudent to tamper. She retained a form of tonsure which had long ago been condemned. She kept Easter at the date formerly established by St. Leo, which had since been abandoned. Like the Russians to-day she kept to her "old style," and was unwilling to give it up. She also retained certain peculiar prayers and ceremonies in the liturgy of the Mass, the administration of baptism, the ordination of clerics, and the consecration of bishops. None of these differences extended to essentials, or were such as exceeded the lawful variations at all times recognized by the Church.

Later on those who held for the Roman uses thoroughly lost their tempers under the resistance they encountered from the British Church in their efforts to coerce her into uniformity. Blinded with passion, these men smelt heresy in practices which St. Gregory and St. Augustine would perhaps have regarded as local uses such as might well be tolerated. Thus the Celtic tonsure became the sign of

* This remark supposes the truth of certain theories broached by the Abbé Duchesne, which can in no way be regarded as conclusively established.

Simon the magician, and the partisans of the old style of reckoning Easter were looked upon as quartodeciman heretics. But the liturgical difficulty would have signified little had it not been complicated by motives of patriotism.

III

IT was in British patriotism that the difficulty lay; indeed, it was to prove insurmountable, though, unhappily, Augustine never suspected it.

In the latter years of the sixth century the Anglo-Saxon conquest had been checked. It seemed likely that at length the hitherto divided Britons would confederate; for several creditable victories had rewarded certain campaigns in which they had combined. They had even won back the valleys of the upper Severn. Moreover, in the north St. Columba's friend, good king Aedhan, had resisted successfully the inroads of the Angles from Northumbria. Unfortunately the alliance was not destined to last. The Britons had hitherto retained possession of a long strip of territory stretching from Edinburgh down to Dorchester; but this was now cut through at two or three different points. First the Saxons in the south cut off Cornwall; then, in 603, at the very time when Augustine came to beg the Britons to aid him in winning the English to the faith, Aedhan was beaten at Dægsastan by the terrible Ethelfrith, and thus another division was effected in the north.

Wales and the other Celtic provinces were in a pitiable condition. Divided both by inroads of the enemy and by internal quarrels, they were losing day by day whatever energy and strength were left to them. Their chieftains were no better than barbarians; they were avaricious, cruel and licentious. Christianity had lapsed into superstition, and chaos reigned alike in Church and state.

What chance of success had St. Augustine? To the

Welsh he did not even represent the Church of Rome—he was merely bishop of the English. Be it well understood that the question of use was in itself of little moment; it served as a pretext, nothing more. The real obstacle to unity was race-hatred. To receive Augustine as their primate would be to accept their present status as final; to renounce for ever their dreams of independence; to bow their necks to the Saxon yoke. To acknowledge that the seat of ecclesiastical authority lay with the English seemed to draw with it as a fatal consequence the recognition of their political supremacy.

Surely there was enough to explain—I do not say to justify—the conduct of the Britons. Many years later the differences in ritual vanished, and schism ceased; but even then the hope of a Welsh restoration still lived on. The Welshman deemed himself to be sprung from a superior race, and would have no alliance with a foreign power. He still fostered the belief that one day he would win back his ancestral soil, when king Arthur should wake again from his long sleep. In the thirteenth century such hopes still lingered. The bards helped to perpetuate the tradition, and it was believed that at the last day the Welsh alone, as sole possessors of the island of Britain, would have to answer for their country before the supreme Judge.

So the evils which beset them had blinded the judgment of that unhappy and vanquished nation. They could not see that they must submit to their lot. Their want of zeal for the conversion of the English was by no means common to their race; for their brethren the Scots from Ireland were preaching the faith throughout Europe, and St. Columba in his monasteries in Scotland was willing to receive converts from the Anglo-Saxons. But history has no record of any Welsh or Cumbrian missionaries. The Saxon invasion hemmed them in as by a wall of iron, and the poor natives gradually exchanged the natural melancholy of their race for a certain fierce mistrust which they have not yet quite lost.

At a time when there remained some hope of the Welsh preserving their independence, since they still held the passes on their mountain-frontier, a council at Caerleon, at which St. David presided, had passed the following decree. It seemed to justify in anticipation the perversity of the British bishops in declining to abandon their schism. "Those who shall act as guides to the barbarians," ran the decree, "shall do thirteen years penance, if there follow neither massacre of Christians, nor bloodshed, nor captivity; otherwise their penance shall last their whole life long, and they shall no longer carry arms." *

IV

WHEN AUGUSTINE had reached the Welsh border, he issued an invitation to a conference. This was addressed to the bishops and doctors; but we do not know for certain whether the bishops responded. Bede speaks only of *sacerdotes*. † Perhaps this is meant to include the bishops, but it may have been that the prelates through prudence or mistrust were unwilling to

* Haddan and Stubbs, *Councils*, i. 118.
† *Oblatus Brettonum sacerdotibus.* Canon Mason in his *Mission of St. Augustine* translates the word in this and other passages as "bishops." When, however, in Gregory's reply to Augustine on the question of jurisdiction, the pope extends his primacy over *omnes Brittaniæ sacerdotes*, the canon reads it as "priests," although Mr. Plummer (*Bede*, ii. p. 55) selects this very passage as one of the cases where it "certainly" means bishops. The fact is that it is not true to say that "*sacerdotes* means bishops." It is a generic term in Bede, as it was in Anglo-Saxon, and in the plural means collectively the *clergy*, which may and often does include the bishops. *Preost* in Anglo-Saxon need not mean more than cleric or ecclesiastic; a priest was *mæsse preost*.

compromise themselves by rashly entering into negotiations with an ally of the English. Or it is possible that our saint's letter only penetrated to certain districts which were still without bishops.

The synod took place under an oak-tree in the territory of the Hwiccas, a Saxon people, who, however, had lately fought against Wessex in alliance with the Welsh. "Augustine," says Bede, "began to exhort them with brotherly admonition to live with him in Catholic peace and to labour with him in preaching the gospel to the heathen for the Lord's sake." His request was simple enough. He seems to have said nothing about his authority as primate, nothing about the question of ritual. He only proposed that they should work for the conversion of the heathen—but work together, united in charity.

Yet even this was a stumbling-block to the Welsh. That they should have any relationship of love or charity with the Saxon was not even to be thought of. They might form alliances with them in their struggles of tribe against tribe; but to stretch the precept of loving one's enemies so far as to help to save their souls seems to have been too much to hope for.

They dared not directly refuse their help; so they turned to other matters. They understood at once what communion with the Roman missionaries would bring upon them. Perhaps they were conscious that their uses were regarded with disfavour on the continent, and that councils had many times over condemned their reckoning of Easter. So they waived the question of the Saxon mission and declared that they could not abandon the practices of their ancestors.

Augustine followed them on to this new ground "with prayers, exhortations and reproofs," says Bede. The monks joined in his entreaties. They pointed out how unreasonable it was for the Celts to hold aloof and set their private inclinations against the practice of the whole Church. The Britons would not listen. It seems likely that there were Saxons in the crowd, and these were doubtless little edified by the quarrel. At length, wearied by the debate, Augustine sought to bring it to a close. Yielding to an inspiration of the Holy Spirit, he said: "Let us pray God, who maketh man to be of one mind in His Father's house, that He may vouchsafe to make known to us by heavenly signs what tradition to follow, and by what way we should strive to enter into His Father's kingdom. Let some sick man be brought in, and whoso by his prayers shall heal him, let us believe that his faith and work are devoted to God and to be followed by all."

The Britons consented though with reluctance. A blind man of English birth was led before them. He was presented to the British priests, who however could not heal him. Then Augustine knelt down, and besought God to render to the blind man his sight and by doing so to shed light into the hearts of those perverse men. The man was healed, and Augustine was hailed as the true herald of the Supreme Light. The Britons were confounded, and acknowledged that Augustine preached the way of justice; but when it became necessary to speak on the matter of use, they declared that they could not abandon their ancient customs without consent and sanction of their fellows. They therefore asked for another conference, which Augustine granted.

V

THE news that a second conference was to take place caused something of a stir in all parts of Wales. People flocked from great distances. The great convent of Bangor y Coed is said to have sent the most learned of its monks with their abbot Dinoth at their head. These were accompanied by a great number of clergy and by seven bishops. The later chronicles state also that several Picts and Irish were present.

Who were these bishops, and what were their sees? How comes it that Bede knows nothing of their names, although he was acquainted with that of abbot Dinoth? Why were the monks of Bangor afterwards punished for their abbot's perversity, whereas no mention is made of chastisement having overtaken the bishops? Who was this abbot Dinoth, whose name is not met with in the *Annales Cambriæ*, although they mention a prince of the name who died in 595? Is it not likely that the alleged abbot was no other than the prince brought back to life for the occasion? The question would perhaps not have suggested itself had not our historian, as though to invite us to mistrust, himself used phrases expressing doubt—*ut perhibent, narratur, fertur*. He is relating old traditions dating from a hundred years back or more, which had become encrusted with such exaggeration and perversion as Saxon malice could not fail to suggest. It is painful to see from his narrative with what antipathy Bede himself regarded the unhappy Britons, for let us remember that they were martyrs for their country, if not indeed for the faith.

It is said that before going to the second conference the seven bishops sought counsel from one of those hermits who dwelt in such great numbers among the Welsh mountains. He whom they consulted enjoyed a high reputation for saintliness and wisdom. "Ought we," they enquired, "to forsake our traditions for the teaching of Augustine?"

It was a strange course to take. As guardians of the faith it was the bishops' duty to examine into the matter by the light of reason aided by grace—not to ask for a sign which should free them from the responsibility of such enquiry.

The hermit answered:

"If Augustine be a man of God, follow him."

"And how may we put this to the test," asked the bishops.

"The Lord saith: *Take up My yoke and learn of Me, for I am meek and humble of heart*. If Augustine be meek and humble of heart, you may believe that he both bears the yoke of Christ himself and is offering it to you to bear. But if he have not meekness, but pride, it is clear that he is not of God, and that we need not heed what he says."

The bishops had better have been satisfied with this answer as it stood; for the sign the hermit suggested, if not conclusive, might at least have served a good purpose. But they wanted something more precise and asked how they might recognize whether Augustine were truly meek and humble.

"Bring it about," replied the hermit, "that he himself with his followers arrive at the place of meeting first, and if, as you draw near, he rise, know that he is a servant of Christ and listen to him with deference. But if he slight you and will not rise in your presence, even though you be the greater number, then do you also slight him."

The test was simple; but it was a superstitious tempting of Providence to make their decision in so grave a matter rest on such a trifle. The conference, if it really took place, shows that the Welsh bishops were as foolish as they were ignorant.

It happened that Augustine remained seated when the prelates came up. "When they saw this," says Bede, "they straightway (*mox*) became angry, and convinced of his pride, sought to gainsay whatever he said." From their quickness to take offence, it is clear that they were already in an angry mood when they came; and inasmuch as they would not listen to what Augustine had to urge, so far from convicting the saint of arrogance, they convict themselves of bad faith.

Why did St. Augustine keep his seat? He acted *more Romano*, says one chronicler; others say that since he was to preside at the conference, he naturally would not rise. It may also be urged that the bishops probably had nothing to distinguish them, being clad like simple monks and without the mitre or episcopal staff, which in those days had not come into use. It is possible to suggest a hundred different reasons, but none of them are much to the purpose. The fact remains that Augustine blundered, as is shown by the lamentable result. Many Protestant historians, who take the side of the Welsh, noisily applaud the issue of the conference, without giving a thought to the question whether any such conference ever really took place.

"Almost every personal trait which is recorded of him," wrote Dean Stanley of our saint,* "shows us that he was not a man of any great elevation of character—that he was often thinking of himself, or of his order, when we should have wished him to be thinking of the great cause he had in hand. We see this in his drawing back from his journey in France; we see it in the additional power which he claimed [!] from Gregory over his own companions; we see it in the warnings sent to him by Gregory, that he was not to be puffed up by the wonders he had wrought in Britain; we see it in the haughty severity with which he treated the remnant of British Christians in Wales, not rising when they approached, and uttering that malediction against them, which sanctioned, if it did not instigate, their massacre by the Saxons; we see it in the legends which grew up after his death."

"Though he be commonly called Augustine the less,"

* *Memorials of Canterbury*, pp. 52, 53.

says Fuller, " in distinction from his namesake Father St. Augustine of Hippo, yet may he be allowed Augustine the great if a measure be taken from the dimensions of his pride and haughtiness."*

So Augustine had lost the battle ere yet it had begun. However, he laid the question before the bishops in the following words :

"In many things you act contrary to our use, nay, to that of the Church universal. Yet if you are willing to submit to me in these three things, that you keep Easter at its proper season, fulfil the ministry of baptism, by which we are born anew to God, after the manner of the holy Roman and apostolic Church, and join us in preaching the Lord's word to the English nation, we will gladly tolerate whatever else you do, although it be contrary to our manner."

Perhaps Augustine sought to show, by a proof stronger than any conventional mark of courtesy would have afforded, that he was not the overbearing and intolerant prelate that they imagined. It is worthy of remark that at this second conference as at the first he appears to have said nothing of his rank as primate. He asked for concurrence not for submission from the British bishops. The rest would have followed as a natural result of union in their missionary labours. Had they lent their help in preaching the gospel to the English, it would have been necessary for both parties to baptize according to the same rite and to keep the Church's festivals at the same date for fear of giving scandal to their converts.

It is likely, however, that they already knew the jurisdiction which the pope had given Augustine. Fearing, therefore, that he would suppress the primatial or metropolitan sees which already existed amongst them, they refused to comply with his demands. They replied that

* *The Church History of Britain*, i. 92. (London, 1842.)

they would do none of these things, and would not have him for archbishop; saying one to another that " if even now he would not rise to us, how much more will he despise us as naught if we begin to be subject to him."*
Then the abbot of Bangor spoke: " We will not preach the faith to that cruel race of strangers who have treacherously driven our ancestors from their country, and robbed their posterity of their inheritance."†

If any credit is to be given to a Welsh document discovered in the seventeenth century and regarded as spurious even by most Protestant writers on the subject, Dinoth could not restrain his passion, and cried out: " Be it known and without doubt unto you, that we all are, and every one of us, obedient and subjects to the Church of God, and to the pope of Rome, and to every godly Christian, to love every one in his degree in perfect charity, and to help every one of them by word and deed to be the children of God; and other obedience than this I do not know due to him whom you name to be pope, nor to be the father of fathers, to be claimed and to be demanded. And this obedience we are ready to give, and to pay to him, and to every Christian continually. Besides, we are under the government of the bishop of Caerleon upon Usk, who is to oversee under God over us, to cause us to keep the way spiritual." ‡

Spurious and inconsistent though the text be, it describes well what is likely to have been in the minds of those poor British priests and bishops, who felt the ground slipping from beneath their feet, and whom anger would naturally have led into such exaggerated language as they would

* Bede, ii. 2.
† This speech is based on Welsh tradition. Cf. Cardinal Moran's *Irish Saints in Great Britain*, pp. 215, 216.
‡ Fuller, *Church History of Britain*, i. 89, 90; Haddan and Stubbs, *Councils*, i. p. 122.

not have used when masters of themselves. Their rejection of Augustine, bishop of the English, was only a step removed from revolt against the pope who gave him his commission; but had they rejected Gregory himself as they rejected Augustine, it would still be difficult to see how the quarrel would furnish any consistent argument in favour of Anglicanism.

The conference speedily broke up. It closed with words of prophetic warning from Augustine:

"If you will not have peace from brethren, you shall have war from foes. If you will not preach to the English nation the way of life, at their hands shall you meet the vengeance of death."

And by divine judgment it was all done as he had foretold; for a few years afterwards the fierce Ethelfrith came and slew the monks of Bangor.

Alas! the conference was only the first scene in a struggle that lasted for centuries, during which charity received many a deep wound. Later the wreckage of the British Church drifted gradually towards Canterbury and Rome. First, in 704, Cumbria adopted the Roman Easter; then, in the second half of the same century, the Welsh sees, and lastly Cornwall, in the ninth century, under archbishop Ceolnoth, each in turn abandoned the schism. Meanwhile, as is witnessed by the following letter, written by an English monk, passion still ran high a hundred years after Augustine had been rejected by British bishops.

"Here is a point contrary to Catholic faith and to gospel tradition. Beyond the Severn the priests of Demetia, though proud of the purity of their lives, hold our communion in such abomination that they will not even consent to pray in the churches with us or deign to eat in token of charity from the same dish as we do. Moreover, what dish or meat is left, they throw to dogs and swine. Vessels and bottles they wash with sand or cinders. They never give us the kiss of peace or the embrace of brotherly love, according to the saying of the Apostle: *Salute one another with an holy kiss;* they do not offer us water to wash our hands or feet. . . But if any of ours, that is the Catholics, seek a lodging from them, they do not deign to take them in till they have done forty days penance."*

Unhappily the Britons were the more disposed to cling obstinately to their schism by reason of the arrogance and malice of the English. We know how unyielding St. Wilfrid of York proved himself, and, although St. Theodore was rather more conciliatory, he yet went so far as to declare the consecration which St. Chad had received from the English bishop Wini to be null, because in the then disorganized condition of the English Church, the see of Canterbury being vacant, the two assistant bishops had been British. Then he consecrated Chad afresh to fill the newly founded see of Lichfield.

This unhappy jealousy lingered till the time of the great persecution of Catholics under Elizabeth, when the English college at Rome was nearly being closed because it was difficult to find students who were willing to submit to a Welsh superior. Although St. Augustine's advances to the Welsh had met with failure, yet when in later years peace was restored between the two Churches, the Britons were unwilling to acknowledge that their position had ever been schismatical, or had ever tended to become so. The *Liber Landavensis* tells us that St. Oudoceus went to Canterbury for consecration; and Urban, a successor in his see, on making a solemn requisition to pope Callistus II. in 1119, protested that the prelates of Llandaff " had been always subject and obedient in all things to the archbishop

* Letter of St. Aldhelm to Geraint, Haddan and Stubbs, *Councils*, iii. 271.

of Canterbury."* The old chroniclers' fancy completely ran away with them, for, throwing probability to the winds, they made Augustine travel so far as Ireland, to the court of good king Colman, where according to the legend he baptized the young prince Levin, who became bishop and was martyred in Germany.

It may be that resistance did not come from the entire Welsh hierarchy, and that there were some less bigoted than the rest who were willing to submit to the authority of Rome. But so tangled is the history of the British Church at that period that it is impossible to separate the few threads of truth from the mass of conflicting legend.

* Liber Landavensis. Haddan and Stubbs, *Councils*, i. 309.

Chapter VII—AUGUSTINE'S LAST YEARS AND DEATH

I

SO AUGUSTINE once more returned to the English. "They at least," says Goscelin, "did not weary him by their word-splitting and verbosity." Five years had elapsed since the mission in England began. Kent was converted, or nearly so. It is uncertain how far the missionaries had penetrated the forests which bounded Kent on the only side not open to the sea; but they probably thought it more prudent to firmly establish the faith in that kingdom before going further afield. They followed the method practised in all ages by the children of St. Benedict, and still observed especially by the Trappists—a method which works slowly perhaps, and requires many workers, but is at least sure and abiding in its results. First a monastery is built; and then while some of the monks go out to preach and catechize, others share the daily life and toil of the country people around, instructing them by their example and thus bit by bit fitting them for the faith. The humble life led by these monks contributed even to the material prosperity of the country round; for clearings were made in Kentish forests, and families began to gather round the monasteries and priories. It is even said that the cultivation of the vine, which for long flourished in the south of England and especially in Kent, was first introduced by the Italian monks. Moreover, when the monkish builders saw the clumsy attempts made by the Saxons to copy the Roman buildings which were still standing amongst them, they taught them some of the secrets of their craft.

Of the missions themselves we have no trustworthy information. Goscelin tells of an old man, even in his day, as we gather, long since dead, whose grandfather had seen St. Augustine. The chronicler is well advised in warning us that the old man's family was remarkable for long life; however, we give the story just as it has come down to us. This man's grandfather was very young when he knew Augustine, whom the people followed about as though he were an angel. The youth used to scoff and sneer at the miracles of which he was told. One day, however, when in the very thick of the crowd, as he was marking the saint's gestures and words that he might turn them to ridicule, he was seized with awe at the sight of his kind, fatherly face. Augustine looked earnestly at him. "Bring that youth hither," he said. He came trembling, and fell at the bishop's feet. Augustine gently reproached him, instructed him in the faith, tenderly embraced him, and after baptizing him promised the gift of long life to his descendants. "Augustine," added the old man, "had the stately mien of a great noble; he was tall and straight, like Saul of old, and stood head and shoulders above the crowd. In appearance he was winning and commanding. He always went about on foot, and often without shoes."

In spite of the miracles which attended his preaching, there were great obstacles to overcome. The people were grossly superstitious. St. Theodore* enjoined seven years penance to any woman who should compel her daughter to go on to the roof or enter an oven to be cured of fever; and five years to any one who should burn corn at a spot where death had occurred. Two hundred years later practices of the same kind were forbidden by the Peni-

* Or rather the author of the Penitential which bears his name, Haddan and Stubbs, *Councils*, iii. 190.

tential of Egbert, which mentions making vows by trees, shouting during eclipses to ward off impending evil, and also witchcraft and charms. Then there was the evil influence of the *scóps* or minstrels, whose favourite themes were debauchery, bloodshed and rape. For good or evil the popular traditions were christianized; the priests became poets, and would sometimes stop on the bridges after divine service, and there sing hymns, as is told of St. Aldhelm. These few details may help us to form a feeble idea of the work to be done.

A letter written by Daniel of Winchester to St. Boniface on occasion of the latter's departure for his German mission, gives us an echo of the controversies in which the monks had to engage with the heathen. Daniel lived less than a century after St. Augustine, and there is little doubt that as a child he was acquainted with some of the saint's disciples and gathered from their lips traditions of the generation before.

"Do not oppose point-blank," he writes, "the descent they claim for their gods. Let them acknowledge that their gods are the offspring of man and woman, and then show from this very admission that they must be human. Ask them if the world had a beginning. If so, who made it? Where were their gods before it existed? If the world is eternal—an idea to be strenuously denied,—who governed it before there existed any gods therein? When, where and by whom were the first god and goddess begotten? Do the gods still beget? If they do not, why have they ceased to do so? If they still do so, point out that they must be infinite in number, and ask which of them is the most powerful. Thus must argument be carried on, with sweetness and moderation, without ridicule or insult. Sometimes compare their teaching with ours, and attack their superstition as it were from the flank. Make them blush for shame, but not with anger. Let them feel that we are ignorant neither of their rites nor of their myths."

Since Boniface would have to deal with savages and barbarians, Daniel suggests such arguments as would best come home to them :

"If your gods are almighty, benevolent and just, not only will they reward their faithful followers, but they must also punish those who despise them. And if they do it during this life, why do they spare Christians who have wrested the world from them? The Christians possess the lands that are fruitful in wine and oil and all good things, whilst to the pagans and their gods there remain only ice and snow." "We must," he adds, "ever insist upon the fact that the world belongs to the Christians, and that in comparison with them those who still cling to their idols are very few in number." *

We know that St. Augustine's preaching was accompanied by miracles; but we have only mediæval legends to tell us what they were. These, however, bear at least one feature of probability: they imply that the saint's mission was fraught with difficulty; they show that the work of conversion met with opposition and resistance, and that the miracles worked by the missionaries were often retributive in character. Thus upon one occasion when the men of a certain tribe had refused to listen to Augustine, and, seizing their arms, had threatened to burn alive both the saint and his companions, he betook himself to prayer and implored God to enlighten those unhappy people. And lo! an invisible fire began to consume the bowels of each one; their skin dried up, hardened, cracked, and blood began to issue forth. Old and young, men and women, were alike attacked by the strange disease—a kind of St. Anthony's Fire. Then they threw themselves

* S. Bonif. Epist. 15; Haddan and Stubbs, *Councils*, iii. 304, 305. In the above translation the letter is somewhat abridged.

humbly at the saint's feet, and yielded; and the frightful sores were healed, washed away with the leprosy of sin by the waters of baptism. Another time a poor youth, who was both a deaf-mute and paralytic, and only able to crawl on his knees, was met by the saint and healed; but the foolish fellow, on his first visit to the church—probably that of Canterbury—filled with pride at his restored powers, made a graceless exhibition of himself by unseemly noise and movement to the great scandal of the faithful. Straightway he became afflicted once more with his former ailments, until he repented and made a sign to the saint, who healed him a second time.

Idolatry could not long withstand the combined preaching and miracles of the devoted apostles. Before its final overthrow, however, it seemed more than once to burst into new life and vigour. Though the conversion of Kent was achieved quickly and with comparative ease, the unlawful passion of a prince was nevertheless sufficient a few years later to throw her back for a moment into thorough heathenism and to lead thousands into apostasy.

II

MEANWHILE the newly-founded Church was beginning to rear souls who were later to become conspicuous for their sanctity. Of the two children whom queen Bertha had borne to Ethelbert, the son, who was to succeed to the throne, was not a Christian; but the daughter Ethelberga was already being trained in those virtues which afterwards made her the Clotilda of Northumbria.

Of Ethelbert's piety we have abundant and authentic testimony in the charters, acts and laws which have come down to us. His laws form the most ancient penal code in Saxon annals. In spite of the obscurity of the text, which is studded with terms that are not yet fully understood, we can trace in them at least vaguely the influence of Christianity. Every article they contain must have been ratified by the witenagemot, that germ of a parliament in which even at that early date the bishops were entitled to sit. Augustine therefore may have taken part with the nobles in passing those laws.

Save in his conversion to Christianity Ethelbert was little affected by any Roman influence. It might have been thought that increasing intercourse with the continent, where the Frankish monarchy had borrowed so much from the former masters of Gaul, and above all Ethelbert's affection for the Italian monks, would have set a Roman stamp upon many of the national institutions of the English. There was, however, but little of the kind, and that little was wholly on the surface. Later on English kings sought to imitate the imperial court, and one of them even assumed the title *basileus*. Roman monuments were copied; old ruins were dug up, and Saxon artists sought to match with their own hands the jewels that were found there. Saxon seals were coarsely engraved with figures copied from Roman art, as, for instance, that of Durham, which represents Jupiter Tonans and bears the ingenuous legend, *Caput Oswaldi regis;* or Ethelbert's own coins, which are stamped with the wolf of the Capitol and the twin brothers. But the only matter of importance in which Roman influence may be traced is thus recorded by Venerable Bede: " Amongst other benefits which by his prudent counsel he conferred upon his people, he framed for them with the assistance of his witenagemot a code of judicial decisions, after the Roman manner." Augustine seems to have exercised admirable discretion. So far from seeking to thrust upon the nation the principles of Roman jurisprudence, he respected its traditions and merely sought to imbue them with the spirit of Christianity. Of a truly Teuton character was the system of compensations in money established by Ethelbert and his wise men. By a curiously barbaric method each limb was assessed at its own price; thus if an adversary's bone were laid bare in a quarrel, he who gave the wound was fined three shillings; if the bone also were injured, four shillings; for dislocating the shoulder the fine was thirty shillings; for striking off the ear, twelve shillings; for more serious injury to the ear, twenty-five shillings; for piercing the lobe of the ear, three shillings; and so on for every part of the body and every conceivable wound.*

But the following was clearly inspired by the Church. Bede tells us that Ethelbert sought to afford protection to those "whose persons and whose teaching he had received." Hence the first article of his penal code is concerned with theft of Church property, and fixes its *wergild*, that is to say the sum to be repaid by way of fine and restitution. St. Gregory had laid down that only the value of the stolen property should be refunded; but Ethelbert knew that his subjects measured a man's worth by the sum payable to him for wrong done. If a freeman stole the king's goods, he was to repay nine times their value; but if he stole goods belonging to God, he had to pay back twelve times; if to a bishop, eleven times; if to a priest, nine times, for a priest ranked as the king's equal; if to a deacon, six times; if to a clerk in lesser orders, three times.†

We may mention another indication of the same spirit of piety. An old German custom sought to protect the weak from the oppression of the strong by making the king protector of the *peace*, that is to say, guardian to the primitive societies formed for mutual defence. In Ethel-

---

* Haddan and Stubbs, *Councils*, iii. 45, 46.   † *Ibid.* iii. 42.

bert's laws, without explicit mention of the *king's peace*, we find set up, perhaps in imitation of it, the *Church's frith*, or Church's peace. Whosoever committed a crime in certain places, or at certain times, or against certain persons closely related to the Church, was allotted double the usual penalty.*

By such enactments as these Ethelbert out of pious gratitude raised the Church to due pre-eminence in the country. He had already laid the foundations of her future wealth by his gifts of land to the two monasteries at Canterbury. The charter by which the see of Rochester was endowed, the only authentic charter which has come down to us from Ethelbert's reign, shows that in such benefactions he was acting under the inspiration of his faith. The deed runs as follows :

"We desire ever to seek how for our soul's healing and for the assurance of our salvation we may devoutly set apart portions of our demesne to offer them to the use of the servants of God. So to you, St. Andrew, and to your Church of Rochester. . . I deliver a part of my demesne. (Here follows a statement of the lands delivered.) And if any one be willing to add thereto, may God give him happiness and length of days. But if any one dare to cut off any part therefrom, may he perish both here and for eternity, unless before his death he repair what evil he may have done. I have drawn up this deed by counsel of Lawrence the bishop and of my princes. I have confirmed it with the sign of the holy cross, and have bidden them do the same." †

This document with its thoughts of salvation was certainly inspired by the preaching of St. Augustine and his monks. Nearly all the old Saxon charters that have come down to us are rich in similar sentiments. "The goods of earth pass away ; those of heaven are lasting ; it

* Art i.   † Haddan and Stubbs, *Conciis*, iii. 52. (Abridged.)

behoves us then to make those that perish serve to win for us those that are everlasting. Man bringeth nothing when he cometh into the world, and when he goeth forth to another world, he beareth away nothing." "The duty of charity is enjoined upon man by the commandment, *Give, and it shall be given unto you.*" So do the words ever keep recurring : " For the health of my soul," " For pardon of my sins," " For my soul and the souls of my forefathers," "Out of love for Almighty God," "To the honour of the blessed Virgin, Mother of God ; " "As I desire the kingdom of heaven." *

Thus did the holy archbishop and his faithful king provide for the Church's future. The great virtues which flourished so abundantly in later centuries, the splendours spiritual and temporal of the Saxon Church, had their seed in such laws and benefactions as we have described, or rather in the piety which begot them. It was the dawn of a new civilization, the beginning of that long alliance between Church and kings which made Saxon England the island of saints. After Augustine and Ethelbert came Paulinus and Edwin, Aidan the Scot and Oswald, Deusdedit and Erconbert, Dunstan and Edgar, Aldhelm and Ini, all examples of the close ties which knit together hierarchy and crown. The Church can dispense at need with the help of the state, but she never spurns the support of a Constantine when it is offered her; for the good example of the great helps her in her mission by giving strength to the feeble wills of her children. So far as possible, missionaries in all ages have sought to strike idolatry at its head ; not because the soul of a king is more precious than that of a peasant, but because the peasant's conversion may go no further than himself, whereas a king or a sage, an Ethelbert or a Newman, never fails to draw others along with him.

* Cf. Canon Jenkins, *Canterbury*, p. 53. (1880.)

III

MEANWHILE Augustine's zeal was not confined to Kent. That country served as a centre for his work, and at need a place of refuge—a fortress, where the faith was secure against attack from heathenism. Five years had been spent in the conversion of Kent—not a long time for so large a kingdom. It is not easy to determine how far beyond its borders the saint or his companions carried the gospel. If we might have believed the traditions of the eleventh century, they traversed England from south to north.

Augustine is said to have preached at Oxford, where the following story is told of his attempt to establish tithes. A certain lord resisted the exaction, so one day at the beginning of mass the saint cried out,

"Let the excommunicate leave the church."

Immediately a tombstone was lifted up, and a corpse came forth from the grave and went out. He was a Briton, who during his lifetime had been excommunicated for refusing to pay the Church's dues. Then the saint called out again,

"Let him who passed the excommunication come forth."

Then from another grave appeared a British priest, who absolved his unhappy countryman. He was asked to remain on earth and preach to the English, but he declined, for he preferred heaven to missionary life. * The Saxon lord, however, was convinced and yielded.

It is stated that on the apostle's passage through Northumbria thousands hastened to be baptized; but here the legend confounds him with St. Paulinus. Then, according to the chronicler, he preached in Dorset, where he is stated to have destroyed idols and baptized great numbers of people; but here again there seems to be

* Acta SS. Maii, vi. 392.

His Last Years and Death

confusion, for the same is told of St. Birinus, another Roman missionary, who only thirty years later found that part of the country still buried in paganism. It was there that Augustine is said to have punished with that terrible disease the people of a certain village who mocked and insulted him. Some miles away from the same place Augustine, when sinking under fatigue and want, was consoled by a vision of Jesus Christ; then, as he struck the ground with his staff, a spring gushed forth, at which his companions slaked their burning thirst. The spot was called Cerne, and afterwards both a church and a monastery were built there. The miraculous spring might still be seen in Goscelin's day.* More famous and certainly more curious is the story of the fishermen who heaped insult and mockery on the missionaries' heads, and then, as they drove them away, fastened fish-tails to their garments. The legend was well known in the middle ages, and passed over to the continent, where a new feature was added to it; for it was said that the descendants of those men were born with tails, and the French revenged themselves for their defeat in the Hundred Years War by nicknaming their English foes "the tailed" (*caudati*). †

These legends, however, seem to give mere variations of the miracle at Ponts-de-Cé.

IV

OUR saint was now drawing near his end. He therefore chose his faithful comrade Lawrence for his successor to carry on his work, and consecrated him bishop. Seeing how the faith had spread on the Kent border, he thought the time had come to begin carrying

---

* Goscelin, S. Aug., 44, 45 ; Dugdale, Monast.
† Goscelin, 41.

out St. Gregory's instructions with regard to bishoprics, and therefore founded the sees of Rochester and London.

Rochester is now a quiet cathedral city, completely overshadowed by the great naval construction yards of Chatham, to which it seems no more than a suburb. In Roman times, however, it had been a fortified post guarding the passage of the river Medway on the road to London. Under the Saxons it did not entirely lose its importance as a military station, and is believed to have been the capital of a self-governing tribe who were vassals of Kent in Ethelbert's time. The little Saxon cathedral, of which the foundations have recently been discovered, was dedicated to St. Andrew, thus once more calling to mind Augustine's monastery on the Cœlian hill. A colony of monks from Canterbury settled there under the rule of Justus, who was made bishop.

Rochester was never an important diocese. Even in our day the Anglican prelate who regards himself as successor to Justus, Gundulph and Fisher, fills one of the least wealthy sees in the country.* For a long time it was little more than an appendage to the archdiocese of Canterbury. When the primacy was vacant, the suffragan at Rochester governed that church till a successor had been chosen. When a new bishop had to be elected for Rochester, the monks of St. Andrew's went to the abbey at Canterbury, laid the episcopal crozier on the high altar, and then went to record their votes in the chapter-house at Christchurch. It was of this poor little see, which bishops often regarded merely as a stepping-stone to further promotion, that Blessed John

---

* The following are the present revenues of some of the English sees : Canterbury £15,000 ; York and London, £10,000 ; Durham, £7,000 ; Winchester, £6,500 ; Salisbury, £5,000 ; Bath and Wells, £5,000 ; Bangor, Chichester, and Exeter, £4,200 each ; Rochester, £3,800 ; Southwell, £3,200 ; Sodor and Man, £1,800.

Fisher spoke—" Never will I leave my poor old wife for the richest widow in England."

After Rochester had been founded, Augustine turned to London. There much had happened under Providence to smoothe the way for the gospel; for the king and founder of the little kingdom of Essex had taken as his second wife Ethelbert's sister, Ricula. Their son Sabert about this time succeeded to the throne. It is possible that the monk Mellitus had accompanied the Saxon princess to her new home. At any rate Sabert yielded to the Christian influence around him, and asked for baptism. Augustine went to give him the sacrament and at the same time to found a new see.

At that time London was a mere wilderness of ruins. Twenty-five years before the old trading-capital of Roman Britain had been destroyed. Theonus the bishop fled with his flock, carrying away the relics and treasures of his church. If any of the former population remained behind, they must have been very few—too few even to form a nucleus for the new Church. The Thames flowed through the low-lying marshes, hemmed in by wooded slopes, and among these stood a fortified eminence on the north bank, at that time in possession of the Saxons. At its foot was a ferry. In later years the ferry gave place to London bridge, and the fort became the Tower of London. It was the key to England; for Kent was girdled by sea or forest, and at no other spot was it possible to pass inland from that kingdom. On every side of London, so far as the eye could reach, there was only wilderness.

Nevertheless St. Gregory had appointed that city for one of the two metropolitan sees into which he wished the country to be divided. Until the suffragan sees should have so multiplied as to permit of their being grouped into separate provinces, it was decided to establish a bishopric there; so Mellitus, a man of noble birth, who had come with the second body of missionaries from Rome, was chosen and consecrated.

On a small hill, covered with tombs, some distance to the west of the fortress, a large piece of waste ground was set aside for the newly founded Church. It was Ethelbert, and not the king of Essex, who made the grant, a proof that he exercised his power beyond the Kent border. A few years later, in 610, the third English cathedral was built there and dedicated to the apostle of the gentiles. Afterwards at the same spot there rose up one of the greatest churches in Christendom, a monument to the piety of the ages of faith. This perished in the Great Fire of London, and nothing remains of it save the bases of two or three of its pillars, which are still standing close to the walls of the huge Protestant temple which has risen in its place.

The new see of London seems only to have been tentative. When Mellitus was expelled a few years later, no one took his place, and his tenure was followed by a vacancy lasting for thirty-eight years. In 653 another effort was made to fill the see, and the Celtic bishop Cedda remained at London for ten years. Then for three years it was again vacant. In 666 it was held by the simoniacal Wini; and at length, in the year 675, St. Erkenwald began anew the long line of bishops of London. Amid the troubles of its early history Gregory's design was forgotten. London never claimed the primacy, but remained till the ninth century the smallest diocese in England save only the tiny Church of Selsey.

The conversion of Essex must have been almost the last news which reached Gregory from England. In March of the following year the great pope died, having filled the see of Peter for thirteen years. Only two months later, on May 26, 605, according to the Canterbury tradition, Augustine followed his master to the kingdom of heaven.

The abbey church which he had begun to build, and which was intended to be the burial-place of the bishops of Canterbury, was not yet finished; so he found a temporary resting-place in the graveyard of the monastery. In 613, when the new building was completed, his remains were placed under the north doorway. Above them was inscribed the following epitaph :

"Here rests the lord Augustine, first archbishop of Doruvernum, who erstwhile was sent hither by blessed Gregory, bishop of the city of Rome, and, being supported by God with the working of miracles, brought king Ethelbert and his people from the worship of idols to the faith, and, having fulfilled in peace the days of his ministry, departed the seventh before the kalends of June in the reign of the same king." *

St. Augustine's active ministry had only lasted about eight years. The chief events of his career are known to us, but nothing more. We know nothing of his life as a monk; nothing of his virtues or miracles; nothing of his death. We do not even know at what age God called him to rest from his labours. What we really know of him may be summed up in a single sentence—he was a tool of the papacy—of the Catholic and Roman Church. We know little or nothing of the *man;* all that we know is the office which he bore and the work which he carried out. The mind that guided and governed his actions was at Rome; and hence Augustine can never be mentioned apart from Gregory. Augustine's name is thrown into the shade by the brilliant fame of his master; yet to compare him to the great pope is not to depreciate him, for the instrument is

---

* Bede, ii. 3, where the above inscription occurs, does not mention the year of Augustine's death. For a summary of the reasons for accepting 604 as the true date rather than 605 with Thorn and others cf. Haddan and Stubbs, *Councils and Eccl. Doc.* iii. 4, and Canon Mason, *Mission of St. Augustine,* p. 102.

naturally something much less than the artist who handles it. Now Augustine was the instrument which the pope had picked out of a thousand for the work which more than any other he had at heart. What higher praise could we give Augustine than this?

So in the Saxon liturgy Augustine held the next place to St. Gregory the Great. The council of Clovesho, held in 747, passed the following decree:

"The birthday * of blessed pope Gregory, and also the seventh day before the kalends of June, being the day of the burial of Saint Augustine, archbishop and confessor, who, having been sent to the people of the English by the aforesaid pope our father Gregory, first brought to them knowledge of the faith, the sacrament of baptism, and tidings of our heavenly country, shall by all be venerated with fitting honour, so that both days shall be held as holy days by churchmen† and monks, and the name of the same blessed father our teacher Augustine in the singing of the litany shall ever follow the invocation of Saint Gregory."

* I.e. the day of his death, March 12, on which day his feast is kept.
† "Ecclesiasticis."

Chapter VIII—ST. AUGUSTINE'S WORK UNDER HIS IMMEDIATE SUCCESSORS

I

OUR sketch of St. Augustine would be incomplete if we did not briefly trace the progress of his work as carried on by his immediate successors. He left at his death three bishops' sees, two kingdoms nearly converted to the faith, and a great self-governing and independent abbey. Then came a time of trial. It seemed for a moment that the fruits of his eight years toil were about to vanish before a sudden revival of paganism; but so far from proving that Augustine was but a poor architect, the storm served to prove the strength of what he had built up.

It was doubtless in obedience to a last wish of his master that the new archbishop Lawrence once more sought communion with the Celtic Churches, for he would hardly have had heart to do it of his own accord. St. Augustine's fruitless meeting with the Welsh bishops appears to have been noised abroad through the entire Celtic nation. The Welsh Church seems not to have entirely severed the tie that bound her to Rome; but Rome's colony at Canterbury was slighted and disregarded. There is evidence that certain Celtic prelates looked upon the Church of Canterbury as a foe, if not as schismatical; for about this time an abbot named Dagan happened to be staying in Rome to submit for the pope's approval the monastic rule of the Irish St. Luanus or Lugid, and it is likely to have been this same Dagan who when passing through Canterbury refused to sit at the missionaries' table and accept their hospitality.*

* Bede ii. 4; Acta SS. Aug. 4, Vita S. Luani.

Then rumours reached Canterbury of the extravagant behaviour of the great monk St. Columban. That holy but fiery Celt, by turns meek and haughty, submissive and arrogant, gentle and passionate, dictated to popes and councils, bidding them accept his views. Rome suffered him to have his say, but it was felt that unity and charity were alike imperilled.

St. Lawrence and his fellow-bishops wrote to the Welsh clergy; but they got no reply. Then they looked to Ireland, and wrote a letter of which only the following disconsolate passage has come down to us:

"When the apostolic see, as is its wont throughout the world, commanded us to preach to the heathen peoples in these regions of the west, and it came about that we entered this island which is called Britain, ere yet we knew the Britons and Scots, believing that they walked according to the custom of the Church universal, we held them both in great reverence for their holiness. But when we came to know the Britons, we thought that the Scots must be better than they. Through bishop Dagan, however, who came to this island we have named, and through abbot Columban, who went into Gaul, we learn that the Scots differ not at all from the Britons in their ways. For when bishop Dagan came to us, he refused to take food, not in our company only, but even in the same house where we were eating." *

If we are to believe Bede, this second effort after re-union succeeded no better than the first. It is doubtful, however, if Bede's information was true. Facts have come down to us which tend to show that Ireland and Wales were not regarded as rebellious at this period. It is alleged that Terenau or MacLaisre, bishop of Armagh, conformed about this time to the Roman uses. Again, Mellitus, bishop of London, travelled in 610 to Rome.

* Bede, ii. 4.

There he laid before pope Boniface the condition of the Church in England. He was also present at a council and subscribed to certain laws of discipline. These he brought before the notice of the other bishops in England. Is it possible that he went to communicate them also to the Welsh bishops? A church near St. Asaph is dedicated to a St. Melided, and the adjoining village of Meliden to this day bears his name.* As a rule the parish churches in Wales received the name of their founder. Moreover, in the *Achau Saint Cymreig*, or pedigree of the Welsh saints, immediately after the name of St. Garmon or German, we read, "Melyd, bishop of London, ... from the country of Rome." Again, in the *Bonedd y Saint*, one of the earliest and best Welsh MSS., St. Peris, whose feast was kept on December 11, bears the title—how strange it sounds in this connection !—of "cardinal of Rome." It certainly seems likely that there were made overtures of peace of which no record has come down to us; that among the unruly and ill-disciplined Celts there were others who, though they clung obstinately to their uses, were yet less blinded by race-hatred. Unhappily the first gained by their contumacy a place in history, which is silent about any others.

The threat or curse which Augustine is said to have uttered on leaving after the second meeting with the Welsh, was before long fulfilled. War was soon ablaze all along the border. In the south the strife with Wessex raged hotter than ever, and in 614 the Britons were defeated at Bampton. In the north the terrible Ethelfrith was ever drawing nearer. He invaded his neighbours in Deira: then, to anticipate an alliance

* Cf. *Continuity or Collapse?* edited by the Rev. J. B. Mackinlay, O.S.B., pp. 84 sqq. (1891.) It may be, however, that the dedication is not really older than the twelfth century, when the influence of the metropolitan Church of Canterbury became strong in Wales.

between the conquered Deirans and the Welsh, he pushed forward and appeared before Chester. Thither Brocmael, prince of Powys, advanced to meet him. On a hill the community of Bangor, numbering from one to two thousand monks, were engaged in prayer; they had gone there after a fast of three days to pray like Moses on the mountain. When Ethelfrith learned the reason of their coming, he exclaimed: "Since these are crying to their God against us, they are fighting against us, even though they carry no weapons;" and he commanded his army to attack them. Twelve hundred perished, and only fifty are said to have escaped. Brocmael fled at the very first onset of the enemy.*

With the tragedy of Bangor—a martyrdom as well as a chastisement—ended the last hopes for British independence. The three parts of the island which the Celts still held, Cornwall, Wales, and Cumbria, were for ever severed. The power of Northumbria was spreading, and before many years had passed she had raised herself to the first rank amongst the Anglo-Saxon kingdoms. The period of the Welsh saints was also nearly at an end. Of those who are best known to us, only two lived after this date—Winefride, martyr of chastity, "in this unbelieving generation still miraculous," and Beuno, bishop and solitary, who raised her back to life. To render the hatred which the Welsh bore their conquerors the more excusable, their national legends represent Beuno as a relentless foe of the English, and even make his fierce patriotism a title to sanctity.

* Bede, ii. 2. It would be vain to expose the ridiculous charge that Augustine instigated the massacre. According to the most reliable modern authorities he had been dead eleven years when it happened.

II

ST. LAWRENCE found a more fruitful field for his labours amongst the Saxon races. In Kent he finished building the church of the Holy Apostles (613), and translated thither the bodies of St. Augustine, St. Liudhard, and queen Bertha. Ethelbert continued his benefactions, and secured to the monastery its independence. The archbishop still lived the rough life of a missionary, preaching, administering the sacraments, sleeping upon straw for a bed, refusing alms save for his poor, shining before men by meekness and gentleness.

Sabert, king of Essex, showed as much zeal for the faith as did his uncle Ethelbert. Not content with the cathedral of St. Paul, which had been built within his city of London, he too wished to have a monastery, just as Canterbury had hers, beyond the walls; so, some three miles away on the little isle of Thorney, the abbey of Westminster was founded in 610. It was built among the marshes which fringed the river Thames.

About this time the faith was offered to East Anglia, who, however, rejected it. This nation was perhaps of purer Teuton blood and was also more united than any of the other Anglo-Saxon races. Redwald, their king, grew day by day in influence at the expense of his neighbours; and in time so many tribes threw off their allegiance to Kent that Ethelbert's overlordship was at last confined to Essex. A new Bretwalda was rising in his place. Meanwhile the aged king of Kent still retained his moral influence. Redwald, when on a visit to Ethelbert, was converted, and received baptism before returning to his own kingdom. His conversion should have won to the Church a large expanse of country, embracing a great part of central Britain and the eastern counties, but Redwald abandoned almost at once his new-found faith, which had only been assumed out of motives of policy. When he returned to his kingdom, he was easily led by his queen and counsellors to return to the worship of his fathers, merely adding our divine Lord to the number of his gods. Almost till Bede's time there was still standing the temple in which the altar to Christ had had its place amongst those erected to the Teuton deities.*

Then Kent fell upon evil days; for Ethelbert died in 616, and with him perished his budding empire. Essex passed under the dominion of East Anglia, and Redwald became Bretwalda—a position he maintained till his death, shortly after his victory over Northumbria. Unfortunately Ethelbert's son, Edbert, who succeeded to his father's throne, resisted the preaching of Augustine and his disciples; and in morals he was even more of a pagan than in belief. He was subject to such fits of fury that he was believed to be mad and to be possessed by an evil spirit. Soon after he became king, he married his stepmother—his father's second wife, for he himself was son to Bertha. Born and bred a pagan, in this union he was merely carrying out the old pagan tradition. Nevertheless Lawrence vehemently opposed it; he was the more bound to do so since the woman must have been a Christian. It was a case specifically covered by St. Gregory's replies to Augustine. Edbald, however, refused to put away the woman. Then those who had become Christians out of policy rather than conviction, threw away the mask and returned to their idols.† The image of Woden was once more set up within the walls of Canterbury.

Ethelbert's death was soon followed by that of Sabert, king of Essex. He left three sons, who like Edbald were pagans. In London also the faith seemed likely once more to be extinguished; for the young princes, idolaters though they were, desired to receive holy communion with the

* Bede, ii. 15.   † Bede, ii. 5.

faithful, and, when Mellitus refused to grant it, he was expelled from the country. When he reached Canterbury, he met there Justus, who had himself been compelled to fly from his own little diocese of Rochester.

The three bishops had good reason for despondency; for a heathen re-action had set in, and it seemed that the work of years was to be overthrown. We do not know how long their conflict with the princes lasted; but we may well believe that they did not give in so long as a vestige of human hope remained.

Nevertheless this page of their history is disappointing. In spite of all that may be urged in their favour, we cannot help regretting that they were so wanting in constancy under trial. We are reminded of the despondency which overtook Augustine's companions on setting out towards England at the very beginning of their mission. Yet the Church holds Lawrence, Mellitus, and Justus as saints notwithstanding, for their life was hard and they died at the post to which they were sent. The thought, however, suggests itself that the faith would have thrived better when first planted on English soil had it been watered with the blood of martyrs.

Mellitus and Justus crossed into Gaul, there to serve God in peace till the end of the persecution. Lawrence was meaning to follow them. One night, however, when, after long prayer for his people, he lay asleep on his mattress within the church, St. Peter, prince of the apostles, appeared and scourged him till the very blood ran from his body. Then he reproached the archbishop for deserting his flock, which he himself had committed to his care. "When thou flyest, to what shepherd wilt thou leave Christ's sheep, now hemmed in by wolves? Dost thou forget my example, how for Christ's little ones, whom as a mark of His great love He had entrusted to me, I bore chains, stripes, imprisonment, torture, lastly death itself, even the death of the cross, from unbelievers and the enemies of Christ, that I might myself be crowned with Christ?"

Roused alike by the scourging and the reproach, Lawrence, as soon as it was morning, sought out the king, and showed him the wounds upon his body. When Edbald learned that they had been received for his salvation's sake, he yielded to grace, put an end to his incestuous union, abandoned his idols, and after receiving baptism built within the abbey a new chapel to the Mother of God. He also recalled Mellitus and Justus, and did what was within his power to promote the faith.

The Church again flourished in Kent as it had done in Ethelbert's and Augustine's time. Justus was restored to his see of Rochester; but though the princes of Essex had been defeated and slain in battle by the Gewissas of Wessex, London still clung to paganism, and would not suffer Justus to return. On account of its apostasy the future capital lost for ever the primacy of the Church in England.

St. Lawrence died in 619, and was succeeded by Mellitus, who only ruled at Canterbury for five years; for he was already aged and suffered from gout, although exceedingly active in his administration. "He was a man of noble birth," says Bede,* "but was nobler by the loftiness of his mind."

Justus succeeded Mellitus, leaving his see of Rochester to the monk Romanus. His primacy lasted six years, from 624 to 630.

Converts still continued to be made; but the people were no longer baptized in hundreds at a time, as had been the case under Augustine. Rather the Church made slow and steady progress, so that greater patience and more persevering courage were required on the part of her

* ii. 7.

apostles. When pope Boniface sent Justus the pallium, *
he congratulated him on the success of his missions, the
fruit of his persevering energy. The conversion of heathen
nations, however, is never achieved in a day. We need
not wonder then that there still remained idolaters in Kent
after thirty years of missionary labour ; for the only abiding
foundations for a new Church are the graves of her
missionaries.

* Neither Lawrence nor Mellitus received the pallium. At Rome, no doubt, it was judged that the expectations of St. Gregory were being but slowly fulfilled, and that sees were still too few to justify the pope in sending it. Under Justus, in whose episcopate St. Paulinus began his missions in the north, things were otherwise. Cf. Bede, ii. 8.

Chapter IX—ST. PAULINUS OF YORK

I

THE few years that Justus held the see of Rochester were marked by the spread of the gospel to Northumbria. For the third time in English history it was through a queen that the work of conversion was started. We must first go back a few years to recover the thread of our narrative.

A series of revolutions had taken place in England while the sixth century was passing into the seventh, and most of these resulted in the further spread of the faith.

Early in 589 war broke out between Deira and Bernicia. Deira was conquered, king Aella's two sons were exiled, and Bernicia under Ethelric and his successor Ethelfrith, kings of Northumbria, became supreme in the north. At this time, just before the coming of St. Augustine, the little rival kingdoms into which England was divided were gathered into three groups, Wessex in the south, Northumbria in the north, and in the southeast Kent, to which Essex, East Anglia, and Mercia were subject.

Ethelbert began to lose his hold over the peoples under his sway; his empire lacked cohesion—that simple kind of federation in which each unit holds its own place. The first to break away was East Anglia under her king Redwald, who though baptized went back at once to his idols. Mercia followed, and Kent lost her supremacy. Meanwhile Ethelfrith the destroyer was at war on the Northumbrian border with the Scots, who had become Christians, and with the Welsh in the southwest. In the interior the ill-affected people of Deira were intriguing across the great forest of Elmet with the British kings. With them had taken refuge the family of Aella, whose name had so happily inspired Gregory in the Roman market-place.

Then in 613 Ethelfrith by a bold and decisive move gained his great victory over the Welsh at Chester, where the monks of Bangor were massacred. Aella's two sons wandered as fugitives from kingdom to kingdom. Of one of them neither the name nor the subsequent history is known to us; his son Hereric was poisoned at the court of the British king Cerdic. The other, who afterwards became known as St. Edwin, king and martyr, fled from place to place pursued by the Northumbrian king. Before long he found a retreat with Ceorl, king of the rising kingdom of Mercia, and married his daughter Quenberga. Thence he was again forced to fly. In 617 he was at Redwald's court in East Anglia. Here we will take up the narrative in Bede's own words:

" Redwald [promised to protect his guest;] but when Ethelfrith learned that Edwin had been seen in that province and with his followers was living at the palace on terms of friendship with the king, he sent envoys to offer Redwald a large sum of money if he would contrive his death; but he did not prevail. Then he sent a second and a third time, offering even greater gifts of gold and silver, and threatening to make war on Redwald if he continued to set him at naught. Then Redwald, overcome by his threats or by his bribes, so far yielded to his solicitation as to promise either to slay Edwin or to hand him over to the envoys. And when Edwin's most trusty friend learned this, he went into the chamber where he was preparing to sleep, for it was the first hour of the night, and having bid him come forth out of doors told him what the king had promised to do to him, adding:

"'If then thou art willing, I will this very hour lead thee

out of the country to a place where neither Redwald nor Ethelfrith shall be able to find thee.'

" ' I thank thee,' he answered, ' for thy good will ; but I cannot do as thou dost suggest, and so be the first to break the engagement I have made with so great a king ; for he hath done me no wrong and as yet hath not acted as my enemy. Rather, if I must die, let him sooner than one of baser rank deliver me to death. For whither should I fly now, who for so many years and seasons have wandered through every country of Britain to escape the toils of my enemies.'

"So when his friend left him, Edwin remained alone out of doors, and sitting down in front of the palace began to be troubled with many an anxious thought, for he knew not what to do or whither to turn.

" He had long been occupied with the silent anguish of his mind and with the fire hidden within his breast, when suddenly he saw approaching through the stillness of the late night a man whose face and bearing he knew not ; whom seeing, so strange and unexpected, he was not a little afraid. But he approached and greeted Edwin, and asked why at that hour, when others were resting, wrapped in deep sleep, he should be seated on a stone wakeful and sorrowful. But Edwin asked in turn what it mattered to him whether he passed the night within doors or without. Then the other said in reply :

" 'Think not that I do not know the reason of your sorrow and wakefulness and of your sitting out of doors alone. For I know for certain who thou art and why thou grievest and what evils thou fearest will very soon befall thee. But tell me what reward thou wilt give to one who shall free thee from thy sorrows and prevail upon Redwald neither to do thee ill with his own hand nor hand thee over for thine enemies to slay.'

"And when he replied that to reward such a one he

would do him every benefit in his power, the other added :

"'And if he promise thee also that, thine enemies being overcome, thyself shall be really king, so as to surpass in power not only thine own ancestors but all who before thee have ever ruled over the English people?'

"But Edwin, taking courage at these questions, did not hesitate to promise that one who should do him such great services he would requite by deeds also deserving of gratitude. Then the other asked a third time:

"'And if he who shall foretell that these great blessings shall truly come to thee, be able to offer thee counsel also for thy salvation and for a better and more useful life than any of thy sires or kindred ever heard of, dost thou consent to obey him and receive his salutary admonitions?'

"Without hesitation Edwin promised at once that he would in all things follow the counsel of any one who after delivering him from so many great misfortunes should raise him to the height of kingly power.

"And when he that was speaking with Edwin heard this reply, he straightway set his hand upon his head, saying:

"'When therefore thou shalt see this sign, be mindful of this occasion and of our conversation, and hasten to fulfil what thou dost now promise.'

"And when he had said this, it is related that he suddenly vanished, so that Edwin might know that it was not a man who had appeared to him, but a spirit.

"And while the prince was still sitting alone at the same spot, gladdened indeed by the consolation that had been brought to him, but still very anxious, as he kept wondering in his mind who he might be that spoke to him, or whence he came, his friend approached him once more." *

* Bede, ii. 12.

This friend brought word that the king had changed his mind; he had unfolded his design to the queen, who had reproached him for it. Redwald renewed his promises and was faithful to them. Such is Bede's story.* Writers who refuse to believe in the vision of the angel say that the East Anglian king was only seeking to hide his hand, and that while he feigned to be treating with Ethelfrith and finally to be won over to his purpose, he was secretly preparing an army against him. However that may be, he pushed forward his troops across the forest or by the lowlands of the Trent valley, and suddenly appeared on the frontier. There Ethelfrith was defeated and slain. †

Deira at once recovered her independence and summoned to the throne the descendant of her former chieftains. So Edwin became king, and the predictions of his angel-visitor began to be fulfilled. Soon he invaded and subdued Bernicia, driving from the country Ethelfrith's children, who took refuge with the Picts in Scotland accompanied by many of the nobles. Then Northumbria became supreme among the English nations. By an admirable disposition of Providence the conqueror was led by his victory to the faith, which the children of the defeated and slain king were destined to find and receive in their exile.

II

EDWIN was probably now about thirty years old. He was intelligent and energetic, and according to tradition first sought to strengthen his kingdom against the Picts in the north by building the fortress of Edinburgh, to which he gave his own name. He then began a victorious and glorious career.

* Some modern writers suggest with little likelihood that the visitor was Paulinus himself.
† Green, *The Making of England*, p. 251.

His capital was York—not a small city without a history like Canterbury, for under its Roman name of Eburacum it had once been capital of a province; and even yet Rome had not forgotten it, for Gregory had instructed Augustine to found there a metropolitan see. Standing in one of the richest and most fertile parts of Britain, on the great military and trade route between north and south, at the confluence of two important rivers, in Roman times Eburacum had been the most important town in the north. A fortified camp dating from Trajan marks the heart of the old city. Owing to the growth of population the space within the walls became too confined, and the town spread over the plain and along the banks of its two rivers. A road near the city on one bank of the river was lined with the tombs of the wealthy, another road on the other bank with those of the poor; in the outskirts were numerous villas and brickyards. Septimus Severus made it the capital of a province and an important military station. Constantius Chlorus took up his residence there. It was long believed that Constantine was born there, and in memory of that great event the town afterwards counted no less than three churches dedicated to St. Helen.

For many years before the Saxon invasion Christianity had flourished at Eburacum. Its bishop Eborius sat at the council of Arles. Legends name amongst his successors St. Sampson of Dol in Brittany, and Pyramus, chaplain to king Arthur. The last bishop was Thadioc, who with the bishop of London towards the end of the sixth century fled before the English with his people and took refuge in Wales.* Then Eburacum gradually fell into ruins; but at the time of Charlemagne there remained enough to call forth the admiration of Alcuin, who had been brought up there. Within its massive walls, where the churches were still standing, and abundant

* Dixon, *Lives of the Archbishops of York*, i. Introduction.

L

traces of former greatness must have remained to excite the wonder of its new masters, Edwin set up his capital. From the top of the old Roman towers built with layers of brick among the masonry he might have seen some miles away towards the west the outskirts of the great forest of Elmet, which sheltered a British kingdom. There the young king had a wrong to avenge in the poisoning of his nephew Hereric; so he took possession both of the forest and of the country beyond as far as the Irish sea. Then from Chester he took ship in order to subdue the isles of Anglesea and Man.

Meanwhile Redwald had died, and his work had perished with him. Little by little the midlands were acquired by Edwin, till Wessex was the only important kingdom which had not yielded. By this time Kent had lost nearly all her former power. However, to prevent that kingdom throwing in her lot with Wessex, Edwin sought alliance with Ethelbert's son Ethelbald by begging the hand of his sister Tate or Ethelberga in marriage.

Such were the events which led by God's Providence to the conversion of Edwin and his people.

"When first he sent suitors," writes Venerable Bede, "to obtain her hand from her brother Ethelbald, the answer came that a Christian maiden might not lawfully be given in marriage to a heathen, for fear lest her faith and the sacraments of the King of heaven should be profaned by union with a king who knew not the worship of the true God. When his envoys brought back this message to Edwin, he promised that he would do nothing contrary to the faith which the maiden practised; nay, that he would suffer her to observe the faith and practice of her religion with all who should come with her, men, women, priests and clergy. Neither did he refuse to submit to that religion himself if after being examined by wise men it should be found holier and more worthy of God.

"So the maiden was promised and sent to Edwin; and in accordance with what had been arranged, Paulinus, a man beloved of God, was ordained bishop, that he might go with her, and both by daily counsel and by the celebration of the heavenly sacraments he might strengthen her and her company, lest they might be defiled by intercourse with the heathen. Now Paulinus was ordained bishop by Justus the archbishop on the twelfth before the kalends of August * in the year of the Lord's Incarnation 625." †

The reader will remember that Paulinus had come from Rome in 601 with Mellitus and the second body of missionaries. Since then he had worked under Augustine and his successors with great zeal to spread the faith in England. The new mission-field to which Providence now called him was of great extent, for it covered half England. The country was but thinly peopled, and the centres of population were separated from one another by great stretches of wilderness, forest, fen or moorland. If any of the Britons still dwelt there, they were so few in number that neither history nor tradition has any record of them.‡ Philology, it is true, has found a few traces of the vanquished race, but the rare Celtic words that live in modern English may have crept in at a later date through intercourse between the British and Saxon races on the Welsh marches. We may be sure that it was pure heathenism that Paulinus had to confront.

At first the missionary must have found his position a trying one, for he was conscious of how much he had to do. "He came with the maiden to king Edwin as the companion of her earthly wedding," says Venerable Bede, " but he rather sought with his whole mind how he might call the nation to which he was going, to recognize the

* July 21.   † Bede, ii. 9.
‡ J. R. Green, *Making of England*, pp. 138 sqq.

truth, and thus, according to the saying of the apostle, present her a chaste virgin to Christ, the one true spouse.

" When he had come to the country, he strove hard to keep by God's help those that had come with him from giving up the faith, and if he might to bring some of the heathen to the grace of faith by his preaching. But, as the apostle says, though he laboured hard in the word, the god of this world blinded the minds of unbelievers, that the light of the gospel of Christ should not shine unto them." *

A year was thus spent with little apparent fruit. Meanwhile Cwichelm, king of Wessex, had regarded Edwin's union with a Kentish princess as a reason for war. In accordance with the practice of the time, before meeting him in battle, he tried treachery. If he might rid himself of his enemy by foul play, half his task would be done, for then the midlands would naturally gravitate to his own side. In 626 Edwin was holding court in one of his residences near the Derwent at the festival of the goddess Eastre; Paulinus and the Christians were keeping the day of the Resurrection. That same day an envoy named Eumer presented himself as the bearer of a message from Cwichelm. Having been admitted, he went on to explain the object of his mission, when suddenly, rising up dagger in hand, he sprang upon the king. One of Edwin's thanes, Lilla, threw himself forward and received a blow from the envoy's poisoned weapon. Eumer had struck so hard that through the body of his courtier the king himself was wounded. A scuffle ensued, in which the Saxon killed another soldier in self-defence, and finally perished himself. Happily the king's wound was but slight.

"That same holy night of Easter the queen had borne to the king a daughter who was called Eanfled. When Edwin, in presence of Paulinus, gave thanks to his gods

* Bede, ii. 9.

for the birth of his daughter, the bishop on his part began to give thanks to the Lord Christ, telling the king that by his prayers to Him he had obtained that the queen's delivery should be safely accomplished without excessive pain. Delighted by these words, the king promised to renounce his idols and to serve Christ, if in his war with the king who had sent the murderer that had given him the wound, God would give him life and victory. As a pledge of the fulfilment of his promise he gave bishop Paulinus his new-born daughter to consecrate to Christ; and she was baptized on the holy day of Pentecost, the first of the people of Northumbria to be christened, together with eleven women * of the king's household."

The campaign was successful (A.D. 626), and Wessex, after being defeated and punished, recognized Edwin as overlord. Then the whole of Anglo-Saxon Britain became united in a single empire. On returning to his northern kingdom the victorious king recalled the promise he had made to the bishop, but he would not immediately and inconsiderately receive the faith. From the time of his promise he had ceased to worship idols; and now he began zealously to attend the instructions of the venerable prelate. Then from those of his thanes of whose wisdom he had the highest opinion he sought counsel as to what step should be taken. Being a man most prudent by nature, he would often sit a long time alone, and though he uttered not a word, in his inmost heart he communed with himself about many things, and considered what he ought to do and what religion he ought to observe.

We may guess the young king's thoughts. So many mysterious things had been accomplished: he must have remembered his strange visitor's predictions, which promised him deliverance, a crown, and a great empire.

* The Latin version of Bede (ii, 9) does not mention that they were women, as is stated in the Anglo-Saxon paraphrase.

All this had come to pass; of all the Anglo-Saxon kings in the island he alone was independent. Kent was a mere cipher; Wessex had been reduced to subjection. In East Anglia, it is true, Redwald's son was reigning, for gratitude made it a duty to recognize that kingdom as self-governing; but even Erpwald had Edwin for his overlord.

Then the king felt the influence of the bishop over him; he would recall his preaching, and may have compared his efforts to convince him with St. Augustine's conversion of Ethelbert. He would ponder over the letter received some time before from Rome, in which pope Boniface V. reminded him that the whole universe was subject to God, the Father, Son and Holy Ghost; that the neighbouring king Edbald and his people were already baptized, and that the queen herself, flesh of his flesh, was also illumined by the light of faith. *

The pope had also written to Ethelberga earnestly exhorting her to pray and work for the conversion of her husband to the end that their union might be complete— a union of soul as well as body. He had also added a few gifts. With the blessing of St. Peter he offered the king a shirt with a single gold ornament upon it, and a cloak of wool from Ancyra; to the queen he sent a silver mirror and a comb of ivory and gold.

All these things must Edwin have pondered, but he still wavered. Yet he had promised the bishop to give himself to Christ, if Christ gave him victory over his enemies, and Christ had given him victory.

Paulinus was made aware of the king's hesitation, and perhaps wondered at it; for he had long known the impetuous character of barbarians, equally ready for good or evil, and more prone to act than to reflect. Far otherwise had it been with Ethelbert, who yielded so readily to Augustine's preaching. We may conceive one thought

* Bede, ii. 10.

which was likely to deter the king: it had perhaps been represented to him that the religion of Christ and temporal well-being went hand in hand; yet what had become of the prosperity of Kent? It must be acknowledged that facts were against the argument. God, however, sent His grace to help the king's good will.

"Paulinus saw," says Bede, "that he might not easily turn into meekness the pride of the king's soul." So one day, as the king was sitting alone, reflecting upon the matter of religion which so troubled him, the man of God came up, and, putting his hand upon his head, asked:

"Dost thou remember this sign?"

Edwin started with alarm: how did Paulinus know his secret? "It seems," says Bede, "that God had revealed it to him." He was about to fall at the bishop's feet, when the latter raised him up with gentle words:

"Thou hast by God's grace escaped the hands of thine enemies and through His bounty hast succeeded to the throne thou didst desire. Take heed that thou fulfil now that third thing which thou didst promise—to receive the faith and keep the commandments of Him who hath rescued thee from temporal adversities and exalted thee to the glory of a temporal kingdom; and He will also free thee from everlasting torments of evil and make thee partaker of His heavenly kingdom, if thou henceforth follow His will which I preach to thee."

The king answered that he was ready at once to submit to the faith; but he would like to speak of the matter among the princes his friends, and his counsellors. His object was not to rest his decision upon their advice, but to give them the opportunity of following his example that all together might be cleansed in the waters of life. Paulinus consented, and the witenagemot was held.

"The record of the debate which followed," says Green, "is of singular interest as revealing the sides of

Christianity which pressed most on our forefathers. To finer minds its charm lay, then as now, in the light it threw on the darkness which encompassed men's lives— the darkness of the future as of the past. . . . Coarser argument told on the crowd." *

The meeting was held at the gates of York, near a site dedicated from time immemorial to the worship of heathen gods, whether British, Roman or Saxon. There stood there a temple or sacred enclosure, a chapel and idols. The place is called to this day Goodmanham, "God's Close."

The king asked each one in turn what he thought of this new teaching and new manner of worshipping the Divinity which Paulinus preached.

The first to answer was the head-priest, Coifi. His tone was sceptical, and addressed to the intelligence of the crowd.

"See, O king, what sort of thing this is which is now preached to us; for I candidly confess, what I know for certain, that the religion we have held hitherto has neither power nor profit in it. No one of thy subjects has more studiously attended to the worship of the gods than myself, and yet there are many who receive from thee greater gifts and higher dignities than I do, and succeed better in all things which they set themselves to do or gain. Now if the gods were worth anything, of course they would rather help me, who have served them with the more devoted care. So if we find on examination that the new things which are preached to us are better and worthier, let us make as much haste as we can to receive them."

In Coifi's words there is an odd mixture of sound sense and ill humour. Most of those present seem to have acquiesced, for from Bede's narrative it does not appear that there was any controversy. Perhaps the king's own wishes were so clear that no one cared to speak against

* *Making of England*, p. 263.

them. After Coifi another spoke, expressing approval of what the pagan priest had urged, and making use of the following beautiful parable, which is so often quoted:

"Methinks, O king, man's present life on earth in comparison with that beyond, of which we know nothing, is like to the flight of a sparrow; for while thou art sitting at supper with thine aldermen and thanes in winter-time, when the hearth is kindled in the middle and the hall is warmed, though without there rage everywhere storms of wintry rain and snow, a sparrow flies quickly through the house, in by one door and out by another. While he is within, he is untouched by the winter storm, but the short time of peace is gone by in a moment, and he goes from the storm back into the storm and is lost to sight. So is the life of man seen for a little while; but of what follows or what has gone before we know nothing at all. Therefore if this new teaching bring us any surer tidings, methinks it were well to follow it."

It comes upon us almost as a surprise to find that those rude Teutons, whom we perhaps imagined to have thought only of the sensual enjoyments of the present life, were themselves possessed by such feelings of unrest and were conscious of a dark and vast beyond. *

Those barbarians were seeking for the secret of life. When Ethelbert first met St. Augustine, he showed great common-sense strangely mingled with childish superstition. Here we go deeper into the soul; though the Northumbrian thane is the only one whose melancholy words have been preserved in history, we may believe that many more had struggled with the same doubt. Edwin himself during his long hours of silent brooding had been trying to solve the same riddle.

Then Coifi spoke again. He said he would like to listen with more attention to what Paulinus had to say

* Taine.

about the God whom he preached. Unlike the king he was not troubled in conscience by long doubt or hesitation, and when the saint had finished his discourse he thought the matter had been discussed long enough; his fiery and hasty temper urged him rather to action.

"Long ago did I learn that what we worshipped was nought; for the more eagerly I sought for truth in that worship the less did I find it. But now I confess that in this preaching there shines forth the truth which can give us the gifts of life, salvation, and everlasting bliss."

Let us consider for a moment the drift of Coifi's remarkable words. Among those men, reared from childhood on a morbid and ridiculous mythology, there were some whom such fables did not satisfy—thoughtful men who were groping for the truth. Was there, they may have wondered, no one to solve their doubts, no supreme God greater than Woden, maker of everything that exists, eternal, living, terrible, unchanging, who reigns from age to age, and governs all things, least as well as greatest? Was there no heaven save walhalla, where eternity was passed in never-ending strife?—no hell save where Hela reigned, a bottomless pit, ever gaping to devour even their gods?

Bede's account of the priest's words, like those of the thane, afford an insight, such as we can gain from very few other passages, into the strange depths of those barbarian souls. Those perhaps will best understand their drift who, being acquainted with the labours of our modern workers on the mission field, know how often the priest meets with souls of whom he can only say that they were waiting.

Coifi ended thus:

"And now, O king, as to these temples and these altars which we have consecrated to so little purpose, I propose that we curse them and deliver them to the flames."

Then the king openly gave his adhesion to the saint's

preaching and declared himself a Christian. Turning to the priest, he asked who should be the first to profane the altars and temples of the idols and the sacred enclosures.

"I," replied Coifi; "I have worshipped them in my folly; who should set a better example than I in destroying them, now that the true God hath given me wisdom?" He asked the king for arms and a stallion; for the Teuton priest might never touch arms and might only ride a mare, so Coifi chose this as the best means of renouncing his idolatrous priesthood. Then girt with a sword, with lance in hand, he mounted the king's horse. "He is mad," said the crowd, who half expected divine vengeance to fall upon him; then he charged at the consecrated hut, thrust his spear into the wall, and bade his companions destroy and burn the building with its contents and enclosure.

III

HIS mind once made up, Edwin hastened to become a Christian. A little wooden chapel was quickly built and dedicated to St. Peter, that the bishop might have a place in which to instruct his catechumens. There on Easter day, April 12, 627, the king was baptized.

Then began for Paulinus a period of unceasing missionary labour. The slow and steady method followed by St. Augustine was impracticable in this new field. He might not tarry to establish a permanent Church at every spot which seemed ripe for the faith; for, so far as is known, he was single-handed save for James the deacon, a man ardent, resolute and zealous. Moreover, being attached to the king's person, he had to accompany him on his journeys from one end of his dominions to the other, to go from village to village in Bernicia and Deira, and even follow him beyond his frontiers to the palaces of tributary princes.

Edwin was ever travelling by hill and dale, attending to the affairs of his people and administering justice. Accordingly peace reigned throughout what Bede calls, though somewhat doubtfully, his empire of England, and it became a proverb that in king Edwin's time a woman with a new-born child might fearlessly travel alone from sea to sea. The good king had also provided fountains with copper cups from which travellers might drink when on their journey; yet no one would dare to steal the cups. He used to ride about his kingdom, and in the time of Venerable Bede people would still recall with admiration the great king's progresses, when his standard of purple and gold was carried before him even in time of peace, and a plume of long feathers waved from his head.

Paulinus and his deacon accompanied him; and while the king was transacting his business and receiving his revenues, they used to go into the country round, generally taking the course of a river, and set up a cross at some suitable spot. James, standing by his side, would intone a Gregorian hymn or anthem. Then a crowd would gather, and great numbers would be converted, for the Spirit of God was upon the people.

We may trace the bishop's movements from place to place in the royal dominions. On every side are memories of his name—a cross here, a brook there—Paulin's Well, Pallinsburn. At York the splendid minster, one of the finest cathedrals in the world, marks the spot where Edwin was baptized. The little wooden chapel, built in the middle of the Roman camp, was far too small for the needs of Edwin's capital; yet he wished to preserve it, for it was the cradle of his faith. So Paulinus set up around it a basilica of stone—a detail Bede never fails to note—and for a long time the greater building served as a setting for the little relic within.

Then in the neighbourhood of York the apostle may be traced to Malton, a ford on the Derwent, where there is a spot still called the Jordan in memory of the numerous baptisms which took place there; also to Dewsbury on the Calder, south of Leeds, where formerly were seen the mouldering ruins of a stone church, near which a large cross bore the inscription, "Here Paulinus preached and baptized;" to the Swale, where legend confounds him with St. Augustine; to Donafield near Doncaster, probably the Campodunum of Bede, where he left as a memorial of his visit a wooden chapel with a stone altar;* to Catterick further north, to a spot near Richmond, to the Yore, into Deira, whither he often went with the king.

Pushing still further north, he reached the present Scotch border opposite the holy island of Lindisfarne, which some years later the Irish St. Aidan made so famous. Edwin had a palace on the bank of a small stream, at which he often went to stay with the queen and his court. There Paulinus would preach according to his wont, and so great were the crowds which gathered from the country round that the bishop and his deacon would catechize from morning to night for thirty-six days at a time. When the ever changing crowds were instructed, he used to take them to the river and there baptize them by immersion. The pseudo-Nennius says there were over ten thousand conversions, and Roger of Wendover adds in his chronicle that there were no idolaters left in the country. The place where these wonders were worked is now called Yverin, near Wooler, in Northumberland.†

Then Paulinus went southwards. At Southwell he baptized fresh crowds in the waters of the Trent. Lincoln

* Cf. Bede ii. 14; Acta Sanctorum, v. pp. 102 sqq.; Oct. 10.
† Dixon, *Lives of the Archbishops of York*, i.

also claims the saint, for there he converted the reeve Blaecca with all his household. In that town a large stone church was built, it may be with part of the neophyte's wealth. In Bede's time its walls were still standing, but they were roofless and falling into ruin. Nevertheless it was a place of pilgrimage, and a year never passed without miracles being wrought there. St. Paulinus left his name to the church which he founded ; but in course of time this was forgotten, and his great model, St. Paul, took his place as patron.

IV

JUST at that time Justus, archbishop of Canterbury, came to die. During his short pontificate he had the consolation of seeing the conquests of the faith multiply twofold and threefold; another king had been baptized, and a new Church had been founded as compensation for the loss of London. Already St. Gregory's plans began to be carried out, for at York was formed the nucleus of the future province, which only awaited development. Justus died November 10, 630,* and was buried by the side of his predecessors, Augustine, Lawrence and Mellitus.

The ranks of the Roman missionaries were ever growing thinner, for it does not appear that fresh recruits came to them from Italy. The monasteries, however, were peopled with Anglo-Saxons, and native clergy began to fill the gaps; for the Anglo-Saxon converts were not like the native tribes of distant lands where our missionaries labour at the present day. Brutalized as they are

* The date of his death is variously placed by historians between 627 and 633.

by many centuries of barbarism, we must look forward to the lapse of many generations before these races are likely to produce any but isolated vocations, or furnish a clergy sufficient for their own needs. Elsewhere, as in China, where the difficulty is less, experience shows us that for the most part the only constant vocations come from families which have held the faith for several generations. In England it was far otherwise; for the Anglo-Saxons were not as the Red-Skins, neither did they come from a refined though ultra-pagan civilization. Fierce and brutish as they were, their vices, like those of all idolaters, stood in the way of their conversion; but they were also a new, intelligent and hardy race, and by their very nature were ready to submit, when once baptized, to the elevating influence of Christianity. Seeing how quickly thousands of them learned the beauty of the priesthood and of religious and missionary life, the mind naturally turns to that other race in the far east who at the very introduction of Christianity embraced both Christian perfection and martyrdom. How strange is that hidden power of faith which at a distance of many centuries caused races so different in origin and character as the Saxons and the Japanese thus suddenly to aspire towards the same ideal!

Since St. Augustine's death the monasteries of Kent had been filling with Anglo-Saxons. Even the sees before long were occupied almost exclusively by men of English birth. The Kentish Ithamar, afterwards bishop of Rochester (644-655), was already a monk in the cloisters of Canterbury. From every kingdom in the island men flocked to the monastery of SS. Peter and Paul. Deusdedit, afterwards first Saxon archbishop, came from Wessex at a time when the apostles of the gospel had only just set foot in that country.* Thomas, second

* St. Birinus, apostle of Wessex, first went there in 634.

bishop of East Anglia, was born in the district of Gyrwas, in the marshy plains bordering on the Wash. Damian, who succeeded Ithamar in 655, came from Sussex.

Religious life was taking root among Saxon women also—women, be it remembered, of the same blood as those whose chastity and moral excellence were extolled by Tacitus. Aidan was soon to found his famous abbey at Hartlepool for the women of Northumbria, at the same time that Edwin's widow was setting up her convent at Lyminge. Hilda, great-niece of the king and sprung from the purest blood of Woden, was a child of about fifteen, when she followed the teaching of Paulinus. That chosen soul afterwards became the first of those great English nuns of whom it were rash to speak after Montalembert. She founded the double monastery of Whitby and was the spiritual mother of a whole generation of bishops and missionaries. She even took her seat at the council of Whitby amongst the bishops and doctors of the English Church.

That beautiful season, so fertile in saints, was already dawning when Justus went to his rest. He was one of the last of Augustine's companions. Honorius, however, Gregory's former choirboy and pupil, who at the head of the monks' procession had entoned the litanies on their road to Canterbury, was still living. He had witnessed the first victories of the faith, and was now chosen to fill in his turn the see of Canterbury. He was consecrated by St. Paulinus at his new church in Lincoln.*

V

AT that time the faith was beginning to prevail in East Anglia. On Redwald's death his kingdom had become a sort of dependency of Northumbria. Using

---

* Bede, ii. 18.

his moral influence as suzerain Edwin in 628 induced the new prince Erpwald to become a Christian. There as elsewhere the party of idolatry began to resist; the old religion of Woden was not to be overcome without a struggle, and the lately baptized king was assassinated. A short period of anarchy followed, during which the kingdom was lost to Northumbria. The newly planted faith was cut down to the root, but God had preserved the seed from which it should rise again, for a brother of the martyred prince was living an exile in Burgundy. There Sigbert had become a Christian. He also became acquainted with St. Columban and studied the monastic life and schools of Gaul. When after three years of anarchy he became king in his native country, he brought with him a bishop, Felix the Burgundian, who became the real founder of the Church in East Anglia, which Paulinus and his disciples had scarcely touched (A.D. 631). A bishop's see subject to Canterbury was established at Dunwich, a small town on the border of Sussex, which has nearly disappeared. Later on the see was removed to Norwich.

The presence of Felix served to promote peace within the Church of England, for being a stranger to the controversies which since the time of St. Augustine's overtures had divided Celts and Romans, he was able to regard things in a calm and unprejudiced light. The two Churches were destined soon to find themselves face to face, for armies of missionaries were ready to invade England both from Scotland and Ireland. There afterwards came a time when each party struggled for its own views with exceeding bitterness. At last, however, when saints on one side met saints on the other, Bede was able to write: "So long as the Irish bishop St. Aidan lived, each side bore with the ritual practices of the other without complaining; he was venerated by the bishops—by Honorius of Canterbury no less than by Felix of East Anglia." *

Now, however, a spirit of peace was abroad. About this time, between 630 and 640, on the occasion of a letter from pope Honorius, the question of liturgical reunion was broached in Ireland. At the council of Old Leighton the southern portion of that island accepted the Roman reckoning of Easter. The great missionary movement which a little later distributed monks from Ireland through the length and breadth of England was heralded by the coming of St. Fursey to Felix's own Church of Dunwich. Fursey was a monk who, perhaps driven from his country by political troubles, set out to travel, followed by two of his brothers and a few disciples, founding monasteries on his way. He settled first in East Anglia. As he was travelling across England he was stopped by illness and was commanded in a vision to stay where he was and preach there. The king granted him a vast tract of forest land at Burgh Castle in Suffolk that he might found a monastery. There he took up his abode in the ruins of a Roman fortress, preaching and baptizing. There also he saw those visions which have become famous. An aged monk who had known him told Bede that he bore on his shoulder and face the scars of burns he had received from the touch of a damned soul while passing through hell, and when he told his companions what he had seen, a hot sweat would issue from under his light tunic, even though it were in the depth of winter—so terrible was the memory of his former vision.†

Finally he was led by his love of a hermit's life to retire into the wilderness with his brother St. Ultan. A year later, disturbed in his solitude by the war which had just broken out, he again took up his pilgrim's staff, crossed into France, and founded the monastery of Lagny, where he died.

* iii. 25. † Ibid. iii. 19.

Monastic life was now spread over the country. Sigbert brought to his kingdom some of the Canterbury monks to found schools; and it has been sought to trace therein the origin of Cambridge University. From what ranks of the people most of the monks came we do not know, but we read of one vocation of that date—that of the king himself. Sigbert, "valiant soldier, great Christian and great scholar," "was seized with such desire for the kingdom of heaven that he left all things, quitted the throne and entered the monastery which he had founded, received the tonsure and strove to win an everlasting crown."*

He is the first of that line of Saxon kings who in the following centuries sought refuge in the cloister and afforded to the world the strange spectacle of a kind of epidemic of religious life.

VI

THE reigning pope, Honorius I., followed from afar the progress of the faith in England. When he learned of the conversion of Northumbria, he wrote to his namesake the archbishop of Canterbury reminding him of the instructions laid down by St. Gregory in his letters to St. Augustine about the establishment of sees. He also sent the pallium both to him and to Paulinus. †

The pope also addressed a letter to the king of Northumbria. He congratulated him on his conversion, telling him how great would be the fruit of his example throughout Christendom. Nothing was more worthy than to believe in and worship God the supreme King; Edwin should persevere in the way opened before him; he should read the works of St. Gregory, the true apostle of England, and diligently study his teaching, so that the great pope's prayers might avail for the welfare of his kingdom and people as well as for his own salvation.*

* Bede, iii. 18. † Bede, ii. 17. ‡ Ibid.

When the letter reached Northumbria, it was too late, for Edwin was already dead.

Like all former attempts at national union, Edwin's empire was weak. For some time past a new power had been growing up in the very heart of the island. Mercia was the last in date of the English kingdoms. It had in turn submitted to the overlordship of Ethelbert, of Redwald and of Edwin; but, being always in close neighbourhood with the Britons, it had kept its taste for war and conquest longer than any of the other kingdoms. Its third king, the usurper, Cearl, had given his daughter in marriage to Edwin during his exile, and from this union there sprang up an alliance between the two kingdoms which lasted a decade. On the eve of Edwin's conversion Cearl died and was succeeded by Penda, a pagan. This man was about fifty years of age and already renowned as a hardy warrior. He was shortly to become Bretwalda, for Wessex had already been conquered by the Mercians, and Northumbria had lost her supremacy. The kingdoms were now grouped in pairs; Northumbria and East Anglia, both in part Christian, combined against Mercia and Wessex. However, Penda would not have prevailed had he not received assistance from an unexpected quarter. Ever looking out for opportunities of revenge, the British kings profited by the divisions between the English princes, which weakened them at their own expense, and Cadwalla, king of Gwynned in North Wales, sought to avenge the conquests both of pagan Ethelfrith and Christian Edwin. He did not hesitate to join Penda in fighting his fellow-Christians, for they were English and therefore objects of his hate.

The rival forces met at Hatfield, near Doncaster, October 12, 633. Edwin was defeated and killed, being then forty-eight years old. The English have always honoured him as a martyr. The following year Penda invaded East Anglia. That people when thus threatened turned for safety to their former king Sigbert, and made him leave his monastery. Armed only with a staff, for he would not spill blood, and clothed in his monk's habit, he placed himself at the head of his army and fell in its defeat.

The battle of Hatfield put an end to Edwin's work of evangelization. While the Mercian king was invading East Anglia, his British ally was glutting upon his prey. "At that time," says Bede, " great havoc was wrought in the Church and people of Northumbria, chiefly because one of the leaders was a heathen, while the other, being a barbarian, was even more savage than the heathen. For Penda like all the people of Mercia was devoted to his idols, and ignorant even of the Christian name ; but Cadwalla, though called and professing himself a Christian, yet in mind and morals was so thoroughly barbarian as not even to spare women or innocent children, but he put all to a death of torture with the savagery of a wild beast. For long he ran riot over every province, resolving to wipe out the whole English people from the land of Britain. He paid no honour even to the Christian religion which had grown up amongst them. Even as to this day is the manner of the Britons, he accounted the faith and the religion of the English for naught, and held communion with them no more than with heathens."*

Moreover the rout of the Christians was followed by apostasy. Osric, who was cousin to Edwin, had been baptized by Paulinus, and had gained the throne of Deira. Eanfrith, son of Ethelfrith, who had been baptized by the monks of Iona, became king of Bernicia. Then came a pagan reaction, perhaps because idolaters looked upon the misfortunes which had befallen their country as the vengeance of their forsaken gods. The two chieftains apostatized, but were soon overtaken by the hand of God, for one was killed in battle with the British and the other

* Bede, ii. 20.

murdered by Cadwalla during a parley. "It was a inauspicious and terrible year," says Bede, "and still looked upon with horror, no less for the wickedness of the two English kings than for the mad tyranny of the British king."*

What became of the missionaries during this troubled period? The work of six years was undone. The members of Edwin's family were either slain or in exile or in full flight. Queen Ethelberga had gone by sea to Kent, and her chaplain, Paulinus, had gone with her. Whilst she sought comfort with her sorrows by founding at Lyminge near Canterbury the first convent of English nuns, Paulinus, worn out by age and by his arduous labours, perhaps also discouraged and disappointed, accepted the little see of Rochester, which had been left vacant by the drowning of the bishop Romanus while on a mission to Rome. There he remained till his death in 644.

The faith, however, still smouldered beneath the embers of the Church in Northumbria, and James the deacon still heroically kept his post.

VII

IT certainly seemed that Augustine's mission from Rome had met with failure everywhere. In Northumbria, East Anglia and Essex the Church was overthrown; efforts made to join in communion with the Welsh Church had been repulsed; Sussex was heathen still and remained so till very many years later; nothing at all had been done in Wessex. In Kent only two sees and a few monasteries had been founded, while the Churches of York, Lincoln and Dunwich were either tottering or fallen. Such seemed to be the sum of forty years missionary labour.

In reality, however, the failure was only on the surface.

* Bede, iii. 1.

The Church was merely undergoing the trials to which Providence is wont to subject works which are destined to be lasting. It was something to have united the distant island of Britain with the rest of Christendom and to have brought from Rome the seed which in coming centuries yielded so rich a harvest of holiness. Meanwhile there had been given an impetus which brought missionaries from every side into England. The Irish Scots under Aidan filled the north and midlands; Romans and Franks came with Birinus to the south. The success of later years was in a large measure due to the labours of Augustine and his monks. Those who came afterwards to spread the faith in East Anglia found the ground already broken by Felix, whose Church though sorely tried was still living. In Wessex, when Birinus came, the soil was still untouched, but it was far otherwise in Northumbria.

Within a year of Edwin's death, when Aidan came down from Scotland with good king Oswald, the tide of conversion, checked for a time, began to flow more strongly than ever. It would be false to say that the labours of Paulinus counted for nothing in the new mission. Moreover, James the deacon was still preaching and baptizing in the country. Long did the Northumbrians keep in remembrance the appearance of their first bishop, who with his tall but stooping figure, his dark hair and Roman nose, "was a man most venerable and awe-inspiring in his look."* Even those who in later years became staunch defenders of the Celtic uses, like the abbess Hilda, were yet mindful that they owed the faith to Paulinus, bishop from Rome.

God forbid that I should seek to lessen in the least the glory due to the Scottish monks. But Anglican controversialists have so often sought to exalt them at the expense of the monks from Rome that it is well to assign to each

* Bede, ii, 16.

side its due place. Kent, East Anglia, Wessex and Sussex were won from heathenism exclusively by missionaries of the popes. St. Aidan must share with St. Paulinus the glory of evangelizing Northumbria. Mercia was the battlefield of the Celtic St. Chad, who, however, held his see of Lichfield from the archbishop of Canterbury, St. Theodore. His brother, Cedd, sought to restore the see of London, but he had no lawful successor, and it is with the Anglo-Roman, St. Erkenwald, that the list of bishops of that see began again, to remain unbroken till the reformation.

"Can it be denied that the efforts [of the Scottish monks] were absorbed in the general movement starting from Rome and Kent? Can it be urged that the English Church as finally established under the government of Theodore ever regarded them as its real rulers? Missionaries full of zeal, illustrious for their asceticism, preaching by their example even more than by their words, they have been and ever will be venerated by the Christians of England. But those in whom was inborn that spirit of order which still marks their descendants could not long hesitate between the enthusiasm of the Irish and the discipline of Rome. From the year 664, only thirty years after the coming of the first missionaries from Scotland, the Scottish rite was abandoned in Northumbria. The primatial see of Canterbury represents the original colony from Rome. The fathers of the second metropolitan see—that of York—are Paulinus, missionary from Rome, and Wilfrid, Englishman and ultramontane, by comparison with whom Theodore himself might almost be called Gallican." *

Do not let us rob Augustine of his title of father to the English Church. We do not give the name of founder to the mason who builds the walls, but to him who laid the stonework in the foundations; to him especially whose master-

* Duchesne, *Églises Séparées*, p. 10.

mind directs the building. But Rome's envoy has sometimes met with scant justice at the hands of English writers. By many of them he is judged and condemned on evidence manifestly insufficient, even from mere legends. They compare him unfavourably with St. Gregory, praising the pope for the directions he gave, and blaming his missionary for having carried them out. They even compare him unfavourably with Ethelbert, and Dean Hook was so audacious as to say on the first page of his *Lives of the Archbishops* that " the see of Canterbury was founded in 597 by Ethelbert, king of Kent." Such writers will not own themselves indebted to Augustine, and to escape the toils of Rome seek to bind themselves by whatever tie they can to the Celtic Church of Ireland or of Wales. Another writer finds fault with our apostle's methods : he judges that in Kent he was too slow, and that though the Christianity he established there was solid and abiding it was too limited in range. It is true that the same author reproaches St. Paulinus with the very opposite fault : when the first bishop of York traversed the north, preached on the banks of every stream, and scattered the gospel-seed broadcast, we are told that his work was hasty and superficial and left no abiding fruit.*

History may well hesitate whom to believe. Truth lies in the dictum of another Protestant writer : "Rome planted ; the Scot watered ; the Briton did nothing." †

Rome planted; and it should be added that Rome pruned, lopped and trained ; for when the time of struggle, trial and hesitation had gone by, after Gregory's disciples and Augustine's brethren had succeeded one another on the throne of Canterbury, Rome sent that truly great man of the early English Church, skilled administrator and learned doctor—a prelate known to the student of history

* Cf. Dr. Lightfoot, *Leaders in the Northern Church*.
† *Encyclopædia Britannica*, 9th edit., viii. s.v. England.

rather than to the man in the street; a man who defended the principles of Rome as well against friends who exaggerated them as against Celts who opposed them; the saintly Theodore, Greek monk from Tarsus and fellow-countryman of St. Paul.

Chapter X—GLORIA POSTHUMA

I

AUGUSTINE'S chief glory lies in the family of saints of whom he is the spiritual father.
When at the end of the fifteenth century the list of English saints was nearly ended, save only for the martyrs of latter days, pilgrims from every part of the world came to visit the two beautiful churches of the English Rome. In every part of both those churches they were shown shrines and reliquaries of saints and martyrs; and they might read therein the entire history of the greatest metropolitan see in the west.

First in the abbey-church, as great as a cathedral, there was unfolded the record of the early English Church. * At the very back, in the chapel behind the high altar, rose the shrine of St. Augustine, with St. Lawrence on his right and St. Mellitus on his left. Close by were SS. Justus and Honorius, Deusdedit and Theodore—the patriarchs of the see, including five Roman archbishops, a Saxon and a Greek. In place of the first abbot, St. Peter, who was drowned in a storm opposite Boulogne, was St. Theodore's fellow-labourer, the African St. Adrian.

Above the high altar were venerated the relics of St Liudhard and the sainted king Ethelbert. Around the sanctuary were gathered other holy men, not so well known, of whom it is doubtful whether they were publicly venerated as saints. Britwald, to whom England owes

---

* Dugdale, Monast.; Acta SS. Vita S. Aug.

its traditional regard for Sunday rest; Tatwin, who organized schools; Nothelm, the friend of Venerable Bede.

Besides the archbishops the kings of Kent and the abbots of the monastery were buried at their death in the crypts or cloisters. But from the eighth century the history of the Church of Canterbury was no longer written on the tombstones of the abbey but on those of the cathedral; for a series of unhappy quarrels had robbed St. Augustine's of the honour of being the burial-place of the saint's successors on the throne of Canterbury. Archbishop Cuthbert (741-758) was by no means lacking in veneration for the holy founder of the see; for it was at the council of Clovesho, at which he presided, that the feasts of St. Gregory and St. Augustine were made of obligation on the English Church. However, rivalry sprang up between the two great churches in his city. The cathedral was then served by seculars, and these grudged the abbey the esteem in which it was held by the people. The bishop, who had secret designs of his own, had just added to his church a new chapel, of which he revealed the future use to no one. He was then old and infirm, and, as was usual in those days, his stone coffin was already being made for him; but there was nothing to excite suspicion that his end was at hand. Suddenly the passing bell was heard, and the monks from St. Augustine's went out in procession to bear the archbishop to their monastery. When, however, they reached Christchurch, they learned that he had been dead and buried three days. It was useless for them to protest; matters had been so arranged by king's and pope's permission. The blow was keenly felt; many centuries later the chronicler of the abbey, Elmham, inveighed against the simplicity of the abbot who had suffered that "seed of a snake to crawl to the church and slay its own mother;"* for was not the abbey church the mother-church of all England?

The new archbishop was Bregwin (758-762). During the next few years the abbey was always on the watch. At the first news of the prelate's illness and approaching death, abbot Jambert hastened with his monks and a band of armed men to the cathedral. However, they were again too late. By way of consolation the canons elected Jambert himself to the see. He at least, when he felt the approach of death, caused himself to be carried in a litter to his beloved abbey, where he was buried. But he was the last of the archbishops to be laid there.

Two hundred years later the monks received some compensation for the loss they had sustained; for devotion to St. Augustine continued to spread, † and in St. Dunstan's time the abbey received the name of its founder, by which it continued to be known. Miracles were often worked there and legends gathered round its walls. More than one church, wishing to claim the saint for its founder, imagined him to have made some highly improbable journeys.

King Canute was especially fervent in his devotion. In 1030 he made a pilgrimage to Rome and on his return was met by the royal fleet. While off Kent a terrible storm arose, and the king made a vow that if he reached England in safety he would make the saint a gift of costly ornaments and also of a gold band, long enough to stretch round the ship. The storm ceased, and the king, as soon as he landed, rode as quickly as he could to offer thanks at his patron's shrine.

Once before, in 1027, the same king had made a gift to the monastery which almost exceeded in value all its

* Thom. de Elmham, xi. 5.
† Goscelin, Mirac. S. Aug. Acta SS. Maii.

other treasures. Kent had been terribly ravaged by the Danes. Near the spot where St. Augustine had landed, a convent of nuns had been destroyed and the community butchered. This was the ancient abbey of Minster, in which were preserved the relics of its holy abbess, the virgin St. Mildred, a descendant of king Ethelbert, who had taken the veil during Theodore's primacy.* It is remarkable that though little was known of her life, yet her fame almost eclipsed that of St. Augustine. Pilgrims came even from the continent to visit her tomb, around which legends grew up, some touching, some amusing in character. St. Mildred even appropriated traditions which rightly belonged to St. Augustine; thus the rock on which he landed and left his footprint became in time St. Mildred's Rock.

Canute gave the church with the relics it contained to the Canterbury monks. In carrying away the church's treasures, however, these had to reckon with the inhabitants and clergy of Thanet; so they went there during the night and hastily seized the relics, having barely time to get away and cross by the ferry, when to the fury of the people they were discovered. The relics of the holy abbess were pointed out to pilgrims in St. Augustine's church. Her shrine was erected in a chapel next to that of the bishops of Canterbury; and thus were gathered together the first primate and his fellow-founders of the English Church, the first Christian king, the first Christian queen, one of the first English abbots and one of the first English abbesses; and from that holy spot, surrounded by his court of saints, St. Augustine dispensed blessings and wrought miracles on behalf of his beloved Kent.

* Acta SS. Jul.

II

TO judge by the miracles collected and recorded by Goscelin, Augustine was especially invoked as protector of those at sea. Whether these be regarded as historical or as mere legends, they have a charm of their own. They show at any rate how great a place St. Augustine held in the imagination of his clients during the middle ages.

In Athelney, a little island in Somerset, it is said that there once stood a tower from which rose a wooden spire of unwonted shape. One of its beams projected in a very striking manner—the chronicler gives no further details of the blemish. This tower was dedicated to St. Augustine. It was said that the abbot of the place was once detained by contrary winds at a port in France, helpless and penniless; so he made a vow to erect a monument to the saint, if he would come to his assistance. His prayer was heard, and when the abbot returned to his monastery, he at once set to work to fulfil his vow. He was given seven wooden beams for the purpose, but on being measured one of them was found to be too short by a foot and a half. This was disappointing; so they prayed to the saint and measured again, when the beam was found to be a foot and a half too long. The abbot would not have it cut; and hence it happened that St. Augustine's tower at the monastery of Athelney was built in defiance of all rules of the builder's art.

Elfnoth, a citizen of London, and a former pupil of the monastery at Canterbury, on returning from the court of William the Conqueror in Normandy, happened to be in extreme peril from shipwreck. He invoked the saint, who sent to his assistance some of the wreckage, on which he was tossed about on the open sea two days and two nights. At length he was rescued, although all his shipmates had been drowned.

Some of the monks of St. Augustine's told Goscelin the following story. One year about Whitsuntide they were on board ship with many other passengers, both laymen and ecclesiastics, returning from the holy land. Between Constantinople and Venice a terrible storm arose; the sails had to be furled, and the ship was at the mercy of the winds. St. Augustine's day was at hand; and the monks, to interest the Greek sailors in their patron, told how Augustine's master St. Gregory had been envoy at Byzantium before he sent him to convert England. There was no more powerful saint than Augustine in Britain, and if all on board, Greeks, Italians and English, would join in praying, they would certainly escape from the danger.

The feast fell on a Sunday. The wind still blew a gale. On Saturday night the monks sang the first vespers on deck, which was swept by the waves; then lauds at daybreak. "The ship was our church, the mast its steeple, the yards its cross, the sails its hangings; the captain was our celebrant, the pilot our head-priest, the rowers our choir, the wind whistling through the rigging our organ." As soon as lauds had been sung, all save the pilot retired to rest; presently the storm abated.

The English monks insisted that if they continued to have confidence in their patron's protection they would speedily arrive at the end of the voyage. The captain, however, chose to put into the nearest port. Hardly had they reached it, when the storm rose again, and, the wind remaining contrary, they were unable to put to sea till they once more had recourse to the saint.

On another occasion, also during the reign of William the Conqueror, fifteen ships were crossing the Channel, with cargoes of stone from Caen. Fourteen of these were destined for the palace of Westminster, and the fifteenth for St. Augustine's abbey, which was being rebuilt. The fourteen ships sank with all on board during a hurricane. Those in the other vessel had confidence in the saint on whose behalf they were making the voyage, and the captain refused to throw overboard the heavy building material, which was thought to be a source of danger. The saint rewarded their devotion, for the ship reached a small harbour, grounded and then broke up, leaving the beach strewn with pillars and their capitals and bases, and with stone ready cut for the walls.

Devotion to St. Augustine seems to have flourished especially in the eleventh century. It prevailed even among the English colony at Constantinople, where an Englishman built a church in honour of the saint. Ships frequently sailed from Greenwich with poor pilgrims on board, who landed at some spot on the coast near Canterbury. Goscelin speaks of a cripple who, though he had got together means for making a pilgrimage to Rome, was taken to St. Augustine's abbey and there healed. Under Abbot Wulfric (1047-1059) miracles so grew in number that the monkish annalist left off recording them. It is true that in those days many things were regarded as miraculous which, though perfectly natural in themselves, seemed to come immediately from the hand of God. Such was the death of the abbey sacristan, who broke his leg in trying to break open the saint's tomb in hope of finding treasure there. The poor man died of his wound.

III

AT the end of the twelfth century the fame of a new saint began to overshadow that of St. Augustine. As we have seen, the second generation of sainted Saxon archbishops no longer had their resting-place near the tomb of their apostle, and their Norman successors also were laid in the cathedral church. Before long devotion to the Saxon saints had to yield to the marvellous glory which shone around the martyr St. Thomas.

Even then, however, St. Augustine still continued to be held in veneration. At the lower end of the choir of the Norman cathedral, behind the high altar, amid a framework of reliquaries and shrines, rose up the archbishop's throne—not that of St. Augustine's days, which is said to have been cut out of a single block of stone, but another made of marble in the same shape as the former. To the left were the altar and tomb of the great statesman St. Dunstan (959-988), who reformed the monasteries of his day; to the right the tomb of St. Elphege, martyred by the Danes (1005-1053). Above was a tomb of unparalleled splendour, perhaps the most magnificent shrine in the world, that of St. Thomas à Becket; in different chapels on either side lay St. Odo the Dane (942-958), St. Alfric (995-1005), and Lanfranc, sometimes called the Blessed : St. Anselm, modest in death as in life, lay a little apart. The other archbishops of the see lay near at hand, save those who like St. Edmund died so far from their church that they could not well be buried there.

History tells us how the treasures of Canterbury were scattered by order of Cranmer, basest of St. Augustine's successors. Nothing is left of St. Thomas's shrine; nothing of those tombs of saints which in the ages of faith made the cathedral one of the richest in relics of any in Christendom. The chapels are left bare, or else are crowded with monuments of surpassing ugliness. But away at the very back of the apse, in the pretty chapel where the "crown" of St. Thomas used to be venerated, may be seen an ancient marble seat, quite bare and of strange shape, on a platform of rough masonry. To that spot have Protestants banished St. Augustine's Chair; there it stands in dreary loneliness. In front of it, in a portion of the choir raised fifteen steps above the rest, was formerly the martyr's shrine. To-day the place remains empty, for the services of the reformed Church are confined to the lower end of the choir, and the spot no longer serves any useful purpose. At long intervals, however, the Chair is used for the enthronement of a new Protestant archbishop. A single tomb of plastered brick, mean and unattractive, stands near it. This is the temporary resting-place of Cranmer's successor, the last lawful son of St. Augustine, Reginald Cardinal Pole. And so within those few yards may be found traces of both beginning and end of the ancient hierarchy.

It is an odd thing that not a single Anglican archbishop since the Reformation has chosen to be buried in his own metropolitan church. The monuments which bear their statues in white marble are mere cenotaphs. One and all have preferred to be laid elsewhere in some distant churchyard. They seem to have found the soil too deeply impregnated with the old faith.*

From Christchurch, which still rises above the ruins of the monastery at its side, let us seek a few hundred yards away all that is left of St. Augustine's. To the Catholic heart the scene is most saddening.

On July 15, 1538, Henry's officers knocked at the abbey gate to demand its surrender in the king's name. As the monks within hesitated to admit them, two cannon were posted on an adjacent hill which commanded the monastery.† Such an argument could not be withstood; so the abbot,

* Archbishop Benson, however, after his sudden death in October last, was buried in the cathedral, not by any wish expressed in his will but by decision of the chapter. Was this in consequence of the unkind remark which has been made that the Anglican archbishops are unwilling to rest in death too near their Catholic predecessors?

† A local tradition. Cf. W. Gostling, *A Walk in and about Canterbury*, p. 47. (1825.)

John Essex, yielded. With his community of thirty monks he signed the deed of surrender, and thus brought to a close the abbey's long history of over nine hundred years.* The whole passed into the king's hands—church, buildings and grounds, and all that they contained, as well as the manors, farms and patronage belonging to the abbey. The abbey-lands amounted to 11,800 acres, and its revenues to over £1,800 in the money of that day. The monks were scattered, and were never heard of more, so that we cannot say if they kept the faith. The deserted abbey was then pillaged; the treasures which had gathered there in the course of centuries were carried off; shrines were rifled, and relics thrown to the wind. The brass was stripped from the tombs, the lead from the roofs. A little later the walls served as quarries, whence cartloads of material were taken to repair the city walls.

The desecrated abbey passed from one owner to another. After its first spoliation Henry VIII. restored it and made it a royal residence. Queen Mary gave it to Cardinal Pole. Elizabeth gave it to Cecil, afterwards earl of Salisbury. In 1625, in a portion of the building which is still shown, Charles I. was married to Henrietta of France.

The abbey reached the lowest depths of its shame a hundred years later, when a brewery, tavern and dancing-hall were set up on its site. The strong walls and Ethelbert's tower were then still standing, but out of the former was afterwards built the Red Lion inn, and the tower was demolished on the ground that it was in danger of falling. Alas! the very house in which I write these lines † was partly built out of the old ruins; stones from the pavement of the church and from the tombs, as well as coffins of monks, were buried in its foundations.

* Christchurch was handed over a year later, March 30, 1539.
† St. Mary's College, Hales Place.

Nowadays the abbey has been restored in some measure to ecclesiastical use. Portions have been rebuilt, and on the old site a library and classrooms have been erected for young Protestant missionaries.

We cannot but feel grateful for the love which those responsible for this Anglican missionary college bear for the old Catholic glories of Canterbury. In their memorial chapel, above the names of their dead, which are inscribed in marble on the walls, are two bas-reliefs, representing respectively St. Gregory with the English slaves and St. Augustine preaching to Ethelbert. The reredos of the altar bears figures of St. Mildred, St. Ethelbert, St. Augustine and queen Bertha. On the walls is inscribed the following legend, in which the rather feeble modern verses embody the rude hexameters which were carved in stone by the monks of the twelfth century within the abbey church :

> Aedibus in sanctis Augustini, ut Patriarchae,
> Ordine septeno requierunt corpora cara,
> Agmen signiferum Christi, primique prophetæ,
> Necnon Rex Ethelberctus, Mildredaque virgo
> Cum sapiente Abbate, micans diadema sacelli ;
> Simplicitate pia memores scripsere Levitae :
> *Septem sunt Angli primates et protopatres,*
> *Septem rectores, septem caeloque triones,*
> *Septem cisternae vitae, septemque lucernae,*
> *Et septem palmae regni, septemque coronae,*
> *Septem sunt stellae quos haec tenet area cellae.*
> Atrox sed postquam disperserat ossa tyrannus,
> Suaveolens tantum nomen per saecula pollet.

The "ruthless tyrant" is Henry VIII., for with these men, in the words of one of their own writers, the reformation was deformation. They are of the school

who call themselves Catholics, whose pet desire is to have us recognize their title to the name. They long to forge anew the chain which bound them to Rome in the past, but they shrink from breaking the fetters which bind them to the Anglican Church of to-day. May God hearken to the prayer which year by year the Church pours forth on their behalf and that of their fellows :

"O God, who by the preaching and miracles of blessed Augustine, Thy confessor and bishop, didst vouchsafe to enlighten the English nation by the shining of the true faith ; grant that through his intercession the hearts of those who have gone astray may come back to the oneness of Thy truth, and that our hearts may be united in doing Thy will."

* Brev. Rom. die 28 Maii.

CANTERBURY CATHEDRAL FROM N.E.

INDEX

Adrian, St. 171
Aedhan, King 102
Aella 22, 140
Agricola 32
Aidan, St. 123, 157, 160, 167-168
Ailred 13
Alans 33
Alban, St. 6
Alcuin, 145
Aldhelm, St. 117
Alfred 123
Alfric, St. 178
Ambrose, St. 84
Anderida 1, 4, 26, 27
Angers 38, 76
Anglesea, Isle of 146
Anjou 39
Annales Cambriæ 107
Anselm, St. 62, 178
Arigius 33, 35
Arles 6, 56, 57, 76, 91, 96
——Council of 145
Armorica 6
Arians 23
Arthur, King 103
Athelney 175
Augustine of Hippo, St. 84, 110
Aust 95
Autun 36
Auvergne 34
Avignon 34

Bampton 133
Bangor y Coed 98, 106, 112, 134
Bath 65, 95
Benedict, St. 20
Benedictines 31, 50, 115

Bennet Biscop, St. 17
Benson, Archbp. 179
Bernicia 22, 140, 144, 155, 165
Bertha 27, 28, 42, 59, 61, 68, 119, 135, 181
Beuno, St. 134
Biblia Gregoriana 75
Birinus, St. 125, 167
Blaecca 158
Boniface IV., St. 133
Boniface V. 139, 150
Boniface, St. 17, 85, 92, 117, 118
Boulogne 40
Bregwin 173
Brihtric 13
British tumuli 10
Britwald 171
Brocmael 134
Brunhild 37, 67, 76
Burgh Castle 162
Burgundy 11, 37, 161
Byzantium, see Constantinople

Cadoc, St. 96
Cadwalla 164, 165, 166
Caerleon 96, 104, 111
Caer Gwent 96
Cæsar 49
Calleva Atrebatum 4
Callistus II. 113
Cambridge University 163
Campodunum 157
Candidus 25
Canterbury
  Description of 51
  Entrance of monks into 51, 52
  Churches at 59-61

Index

Canterbury : *continued*.
  Cathedral, *see* Christ-
    church
Canute   5, 173, 174
Carolingians   91
Carthage   32, 82
Catterick   157
Ceawlin   19, 27
Cedda, St., Bishop 128, 168
Cecil   180
Ceolnoth   112
Ceolwulf   13
Ceorl   141, 164
Cerdic   141
Cerne   125
Chad, St.   113, 168
Châlons   37, 76
Charibert I.   7, 28
Charles I.   180
Chatham   126
Chester   5, 134, 141, 146
Christchurch 60, 61, 63,
     65, 126, 179, 180
Church's Frith   122
Clotaire I.   29, 76
Clotilda, St.   29
Clovesho   85, 130, 172
Clovis   53
Cœlian Hill   20, 60, 126
Coifi   152-154
Colchester   4
Colman, St.   99, 114
Columba, St.   18, 102, 103
Columban, St.   132, 161
Constantine 61, 80, 81, 145
Constantinople   20, 23,
   27, 61, 67, 68, 176, 177
Constantius Chlorus   145
Cornwall   102, 112, 134
Corsica   24
Coventry, Diocese of   65
Cranmer   178
Cumbria   134
Cuthbert, Archbp.   172
Cwichelm   148
Cynewulf   13

Dægsastan   102
Dagan   131, 132
Damian   160
Danes   178
Daniel of Winchester
     117, 118
David of Menevia, St.
     19, 95, 98, 104
Deal   49
Dean, Forest of   96
Deira   21, 133, 140, 155,
     157, 165
Deusdedit, St. 123, 159, 171
Demetia   112
Deva   4, 5
Dewsbury   157
Diana   84
Didier, Bishop   36
Dinoth   107, 111
Donafield   157
Donatists   24
Doncaster   164
Dorchester   102
Dorset   124
Dover   40
Duchesne, Abbé, 61, 86,
     89, 101, 168
Dunstan, St.   123, 178
Dunwich   162
Durham   22, 39, 65, 120
Durovernum, *see* Canter-
     bury

Eadmer   62
Eanfled   148
Eanfrith   165
East Anglia 19, 135, 136,
     140, 160, 164, 168
Easter   84, 162
Eastre   84, 148
Ebbsfleet   41, 49
Eborius   145
Eburacum, *see* York
Edbald   136, 150
Edinburgh   102, 144
Edmund, St., Bishop   178

Index

Edwin, St. 16, 123, 140-157, 165
Elfwald 13
Elfnoth 175
Elizabeth 10, 113
Elphege, St. 178
Elmet, Forest of 141, 146
Elmham 75
Ely 65
English College at Rome 113
Erconbert, St. 123
Erdwulf 12
Erkenwald, St. 128, 168
Erpwald 150, 161
Essex 127, 135, 136, 140, 166
Essex, John 180
Ethelbald 146
Ethelberga 146, 150, 166
Ethelbert
  Early ambition 26, 27
  Reception of the missionaries 42-48
  Conversion 53-55
  Compared to Constantine 61, 80
  Letter from St. Gregory 79-81
  Relics of 171
Ethelbert's Tower 180
Ethelfrith 19, 102, 112, 133, 140, 141, 164, 165
Ethelred 13
Ethelric 140
Eulogius 57, 67
Eusebius, St. 87
Eumer 148
Ezechiel, Homilies on 24, 67

Faddiley 27
Felix, St. 161, 162, 167
Fisher, B. John 126
Flaminian Way 22
Franks 11, 27, 33, 167
Fuller 110, 111
Fursey, St. 162

Gap 87
Gasquet, Dòm F. A. 66
Gaul 23, 25, 30, 56, 87
Gemot 10
Geoffrey of Angers 39
German of Auxerre, St. 6, 99
Germany 1, 14, 25, 30, 114
Gewissas 138
Gildas 2, 19, 97, 98, 100
Glastonbury 8, 95
Gloucestershire 95
Goodmanham 152
Goscelin 38, 53, 58, 115, 116, 125
Goths 33
Greece 24
Gregory the Great, St. 18-31
  Letters 35-38, 57, 67-73, 76-85, 89-94
Gregory of Tours, St. 26, 27, 37
Gregorian Chant 43
Guenta Belgarum 5
Gundulph 126
Gwent 26
Gwynned 164
Gyrwas 160

Hannibal 32
Hartlepool 160
Hatfield 164-165
Hela 154
Helen, St. 61, 68, 145
Hengest 26
Henrietta Maria 180
Henry VIII. 10, 179-181
Hereric 167, 141
Hilda, St. 160
Honorius of Canterbury, St. 30, 160, 163
Honorius I., Pope 82, 162, 171
Hundred-moot 10
Hwiccas 105

Infangtheof 64

Index

Ingoberga 28
Ini 123
Iona 19
Ireland 18, 99, 103
Istria 23
Italy 18, 24, 78, 87
Ithamar 159

Jambert 173
James, deacon 30, 155, 166, 167
Janus, Temple of 82
Jews and slave-trade 20
John the monk 30
Jordan 157
Joseph of Arimathea, St. 95
Judaism, Relics of 92
Jupiter Tonans 120
Justus, St. 74, 126, 137, 139, 158, 171
Jutes 11

Kemble 32

Lagny 162
Lanfranc 62, 178
Lateran 20, 61
Lavisse, M. 32
Lawrence, St. 30, 67, 68, 74, 76, 122, 125, 131, 132, 135-138, 171
Leander, St. 90
Leo I., St. 101
Lerins 33
Leven 114
Liber Landavensis 113
Lichfield 113
Lilla 148
Lincoln 4, 157, 160, 166
Lindisfarne 157
Liudhard, St., Bishop 28, 42, 135, 171
Llan Elwy 98
Llancarvan 96
Llandaff 19, 96, 97, 98
Loire, Valley of the 38

Lombards 20, 23, 24
Lombardy 24
London 2, 4, 5, 27, 74, 77, 95, 126, 127, 125, 137, 158
London Bridge 127
Luanus, St., see Lugid
Lucius, St. 96
Lugid, St. 131
Lyminge 160, 166
Lyons 36, 76

MacLaisre 132
Malton 157
Man, Isle of 146
Marseilles 36, 76
Martin of Tours, St. 82
Melided, Church of St. 133
Meliden 133
Mellitus, St. 74, 76, 82, 85, 127, 132, 137, 138, 171
Mercia 19, 140, 141, 164, 165, 168
Metz 36, 76
Mildred, St. 50, 174, 181
Minster 50, 174
Monks' Wall 50
Moran, Cardinal 111
Moses 71
Monte Cassino, 20, 65, 82
Mount Sinai 71

Northumbria 19, 74, 102, 124, 134, 140, 161, 165-168
Norwich, diocese of 65
Nothelm 85, 172

Oaten Hill 10
Odo, St. 178
Old Leighton 216
Orléans 36, 37
Osred 12, 13
Osric 13, 165
Oswald, St. 13, 71, 123, 167
Oswulf 13
Oudoceus, St. 19, 113

Oxford	124	Romanus	138, 166
		Rome	6, 34, 61, 62, 68, 76, 77, 82, 101
Palladius	6		
Pallinsburn	156	Rouen, see of	76
Pallium	36, 76, 77, 139, 163	Russians	101
Pancras, St., Church of	83	Rutupiæ, see Richborough	
Pantheon	82		
Paris	76	Sabert	127, 135, 136
Patrick, St.	6, 33, 99	St. Albans	65
Patrimony of St. Peter	25	St. Andrew's Monastery	20, 60, 126
Paulinus, St.	16, 74, 124, 144, 147-158, 163, 165-167	St. Augustine's Abbey	56, 59-60, 64-66, 75, 159, 171-173, 177
Pelagianism	18		
Pelagius	6		
Pelagius II.	20, 22, 23	St. Martin's Church	8, 28, 42, 51, 52, 54, 56, 88
Penda	164, 165		
Peris, St.	133	St. Martin's tomb	38
Persia	24	St. Paul's	84, 135
Peter, St.	137, 171	SS. Peter and Paul, Abbey of, see St. Augustine's	
Peter, St., monk	30, 67, 74		
Pevensey	4	Salvianus	33
Picts	4, 107, 144	Saxon Conquest	1-8
Placid, St.	20	Saxons, The	
Pole, Cardinal	179	Religion and character of	11, 17
Ponts-de-Cé	38-40, 125		
Procopius	18, 27	Manners and customs of	13, 14, 41, 43, 84
Protasius, bishop of Aix	33		
Pyramus	145	Sampson, St.	145
		Sardica	6
Quartodeciman heretics	102	Sardinia	24
Quenberga	141	Scipio	32
		Scots	103, 140, 167
Radbad, bishop of Dol	7	Selsey	128
Radegund	29	Senlis	28
Ramsgate	49, 50	Septimus Severus	145
Reculver	61	Settle	2
Redwald	135, 144	Severn	95, 102, 112
Richborough	41, 48, 49, 50	Sheppey	58
Richmond	157	Shiremoot	10
Ricula	127	Sicily	20
Rimini, synod of	6	Sidonius Apollinaris	33
Rochester, diocese of	65, 74, 126, 127, 137, 166	Siegfried	17
		Sigbert	161, 162, 163, 165
Roger of Wendover	157	Silchester	5
Roman Campagna	20, 86	Simon the Magician	102
Romans	2, 4, 49, 167	Southwell	157

Index

Spain 6, 23
Spaniards 21
Stable Gate 52
States of the Church 61
Stephen, Abbot of Lerins 34
Stephen, King 64
Stone, B. John 10
Stour 51
Sussex 166, 168
Swale 58, 157
Syagrius 36
Sylvester, St. 61

Tacitus 13, 160
Taine 17
Tate, *see* Ethelberga
Teilo, St. 19, 97
Terenau 132
Thames 2, 4, 19, 26, 27, 61, 127
Thadioc 145
Thanet, Isle of 40, 41, 43, 48, 49, 174
Theodebert 37
Theodore, St. 13, 113, 116, 168, 170, 171, 174
Theodoric 37
Theonus, Bishop 127
Thomas of Canterbury, St., 178
Thomas, Bishop 159-160
Thor 14
Thorney, Isle of 135
Tiw 14
Toulon, See of 76
Tours 28, 38
Tower of London, 8, 127
Trappists 115
Trent Valley 144

Ultan, St. 162
Urban, bp. of Llandaff 113
Uriconium 5

Vatican 22, 62

Venice 176
Venta Silurum 96
Vercelli 87
Victricius of Rouen 6
Vienne 36
Virgilius 36, 56

Wales, Early Church of 19, 96-98, 101, 166
Monastic life in 98-100
Walhalla 154
Wantsome 49, 61
Welsh, Character of the 99-100, 102
not missionaries 19, 103
Conferences with the 104-112
Wergild 7, 121
Wessex 1, 13, 19, 27, 105, 133, 146, 148, 164, 166-168
Westminster Abbey 84, 135
,, Palace 176
Whitby 160
Wilfrid of York, St. 113, 168
William the Conqueror, 175, 176
Wimbledon 27
Winchester 5, 65
Winefride, St. 134
Wini, bishop of London 113, 128
Witenagemot 10, 56, 120, 151
Woden 14, 136, 154, 161
Wroxeter 5
Wulfric 177
Wulfstan, bishop of Worcester 14
Yore 157
York 4, 5, 74, 77, 78, 144-146, 152, 166, 168
Minster 156
Yverin 157
Yule 84

www.ingramcontent.com/pod-product-compliance
Lightning Source LLC
Chambersburg PA
CBHW020910230426
43666CB00008B/1393